# Getting Married Again

# Getting Married Again

## A Christian Guide to Successful Remarriage

## Bob W. Brown

WORD BOOKS
PUBLISHER
WACO, TEXAS

*GETTING MARRIED AGAIN*

*Scripture quotations marked* NEB *are from the* New English Bible, © *The Delegates of the Oxford University Press and The Syndics of The Cambridge University Press, 1961, 1970 and are reprinted by permission. All other Scripture quotations are from the King James, or Authorized Version of the Bible.*

ISBN 0-8499-0105-7
*Library of Congress Catalog Card Number: 78-59433*
*Printed in the United States of America*

*To My Friends*
*Bob Turley, Morton Oliver, Bill Burkett*

# Contents

# Preface

Divorce and remarriage are two of the most important decisions a person can make. His or her happiness, self-respect, and religious life are involved in those decisions. I have been a participant in these decisions with friends and church members for nearly thirty years. Any church member, any relative or friend, has gone through the experience of divorce and remarriage with someone sometime.

Unfortunately, we have often contributed to the hassle and the guilt. The divorce/remarriage question is complex. Feelings. Children. Finances. New lifestyle. Religion. In-laws. Surely we can help each other in this transition time. I wanted to write a book that would help the person involved in divorce/remarriage. I wanted to write a book that would help those people who are not involved understand those who are.

I have been honored to serve as pastor of the Trinity Baptist Church, Lexington, Kentucky, since August, 1958. Our church has been open and helpful to people who are remarried. Thanks to those church members who, by example, have encouraged me to write this book. Thanks to my remarried friends who have confirmed my belief that new marriages can work.

Helen and I celebrated our twenty-fifth anniversary while I was finishing this manuscript. She understands. My children, Jeff and Amy, shared my time without complaint. Thanks to my church associates Rick, Andy, Marvin, Jim, Arthur, and Jim. Thanks to June and Edna, my secretaries, who typed and retyped. Thanks to Dr. Barnett, Rick, Mort, Bob, and Bill, who talked it through

9

with me. Thanks to Claudia who corrected, criticized, and contributed to this manuscript. Thanks to my church for understanding my urge to write.

And thanks to our Lord Jesus who set out ideals, and who loves us and forgives us when we miss the mark.

BOB BROWN

# Introduction

When the divorce is over, remarriage is considered. Remarriage was probably considered before the divorce was final. Divorce is an unpleasant experience, but time heals much of that hurt. A new start in a new marriage is an option. There is some excitement and some anxiety about remarriage. That is understandable. This is not a casual decision. There are hopes and expectations about this new marriage. It should "work." It should provide happiness.

When God created the world, according to the Bible account, he was satisfied with his handiwork. As he finished each act of creation God looked on what he had made, and God said, "That's good." God was not indulging in self-congratulation; he was making a value judgment upon the universe. We are constantly amazed at how good it all really is, and the more we learn through science and technology, the more we are impressed with the goodness of God's world.

But there is discord in the Genesis story. When God made man, God said that "it is *not* good for man to be alone." So God made woman. The creation story has a clear teaching about man and woman. It is normal for man and woman to live together. Their relationship changes the "not good" of creation into the best part of creation.

Like all of the Bible truths, this creation account has substantial day-to-day evidence to support it. Most men and women need a mate. In our society this mating is done legally and socially through marriage. The majority of our people recognize marriage as the legitimate way for a man and woman to find the happiness and fulfillment they need together.

Society does not view marriage as a casual relationship. We issue marriage licenses and keep legal records of marriages because this is necessary to the order and structure of our society. Part of the legal necessity in this area relates to children. Legal records of marriages and births help guarantee the rights of children. Society assumes that children must be sheltered, clothed, fed, and educated. They have some property rights. We also assume certain rights and privileges for the man and woman who marry. There is a variety of property and personal rights involved in marriage. We license marriages, and dissolve marriages by law, so that these can be protected.

Beyond the legal aspects of marriage, society assumes that marriage involves some commitment. This commitment is approved and condoned through the wedding ceremony. Marriage is considered by most people to be important enough and significant enough to deserve some form, some ritual. Wedding ceremonies differ within certain cultural and religious groups, but people normally participate in some kind of ceremony that lends significance to the commitment.

This public and legal commitment, as evidenced by a ceremony and a license, is accepted in our society. It is the way that we approve and give some order to the family. It is our structured way of fitting the family into our community. Social and legal approval is important. The church has traditionally blessed weddings by approval and participation.

In this generation, however, the institution of marriage is under attack. There are those who say that marriage in its ideal state is impossible. They support their argument by saying that marriage has always been qualified by divorce, that every society has made some provision for divorce, that there has been polygamy and adultery. They argue that if marriage were a viable institution these things would not exist.

Furthermore, marriage has been made suspect by the soaring divorce rate. Many question a relationship that fails more than one-third of the time. But like all statistics, these statistics must be considered in context. The divorce rate is set against a human contract that ideally endures until death. Not many human relationships presuppose that length of time. Most people marry when they are young; at the present time our life expectancy suggests that the marriage will last for fifty years. That's a long time. The marriage contract must endure social and community changes. It must outlast family and vocational changes. Marriage assumes a personal relationship that will weather dramatic and necessary personal changes.

Considering the length of time that "till death do us part" assumes, the divorce statistic isn't as frightening as it may appear. The number of divorces does not mean that marriage is a failure. The fact that one-third of these marriages fail also means that about two-thirds of them succeed. But what about the ones that do fail? The church has always disapproved of divorce and has been especially firm about remarriage. Can a Christian marry again? Doesn't the Bible speak definitely and plainly about divorce and remarriage being sinful?

Yes, the Bible holds "till death do us part" as the marriage ideal. The New Testament does condemn divorce and counsels against remarriage. The Bible is clear in this area. But there is another biblical theme that is important in this consideration—the biblical idea of redemption.

Redemption has to do with starting over. The major thrust of the biblical revelation is that we all can, and must, constantly begin again. No failure is final, no sin unforgiveable. There is nothing that separates us from the love of Christ. We are always falling short of the glory of God, but we must always be starting again.

God does not approve of our sin and our weakness. He

is not pleased when we fail and err. But God knows that all of us sin, and he still loves us. He is constantly prodding us with his love to get up and try again. He is always saying to us that no failure is final, that no sin pushes us away from his love.

This is illustrated over and over in Bible stories like the story of Moses, who murdered and disobeyed but was still used and blessed by God. David failed morally, but God loved him and used him after his sin. Simon Peter is a lesson in contrasts: the same Peter called "Satan" by Jesus was also named "The Rock." The same Peter who denied Jesus became the preacher at Pentecost. The same Peter who was frightened by and scornful of the Gentiles baptized Cornelius. God is able to use us, bless us, and love us after we have failed. By no standard is divorce and remarriage a more serious, a more dramatic problem than the problem of Moses, David, or Simon Peter.

There is always the hope of beginning again. It is unfortunate that some churches readily, even enthusiastically, embrace people who have failed in almost any area except the area of marriage. We have seen churches who make heroes out of alcoholics, drug addicts, criminals, and cheats, who boast about the power of God to save and start men again, but who are absolutely rigid about marriage. This attitude is the opposite of the biblical idea of starting again. Our religion is based upon the "second chance" or the "seventieth chance." When a person marries again, he makes a decision within the framework of redemption.

I can encourage people to marry again out of my personal experience. I became a pastor when I was eighteen years old. Very soon in that first church, I was asked to marry a couple, both of whom had been married previously. There were no rules in my church that regulated this decision, so I decided in good conscience to perform that ceremony. That was in 1948. That couple is still married and have had a successful life together.

Since that experience in 1948 I have performed dozens of remarriages. I have been pastor of only three churches during those years. That means that I've stayed in each church and community long enough to observe those second marriages. Some of them have failed, but no more second marriages have failed than have first marriages. I have seen enough remarriages to know they can, and often do, work.

There are some obvious reasons for this. The remarriage usually involves people who are older and more mature. They have learned some things about marriage and some things about themselves in the previous marriage and divorce. They have not given up on marriage; they have just given up on a marriage to a particular person. They have hope and expectancy, or they would not even be contemplating marriage. They may be more determined to make it work than they were the first time. And I think they have usually used better judgment in choosing the second partner.

Candidly, I am confident that I would remarry if I were to become single. My personal life has been so involved and influenced by my marriage that I cannot easily imagine being unmarried. There is nothing about being single that appeals to me. I am not good alone. I want to share, talk, and laugh with someone. I do not want to eat alone, or weep alone, or dream alone. I am conditioned to the marriage experience. I am sure that if I were widowed or divorced I would want to marry again. Because of this, I cannot tell someone who is single, whether divorced or not, that they should not marry. They certainly have the same privileges under God that I would take for myself.

In short, I believe that marriage is a normal, God-approved way for a man and woman to find happiness. I believe that divorce is a failure, but the biblical idea of "starting over" is the dominating Bible message. I know that people can find happiness in remarriage. And I believe in marriage and would not want to live alone

myself. When a person decides to get married again, he
or she is making the right decision.

# I.
# Divorce,
# Remarriage,
# and the Bible

# "Oh, I know what the Bible says"

"Oh, I know what the Bible says," Lynn began. Lynn is a sincere churchman who has been divorced for nearly three years. He attends services of his church regularly and has listened to sermons against divorce and remarriage all of his church life.

"I know that God intended for one man and one woman to live together forever. The Bible says that from Genesis to Revelation," Lynn concluded.

Like many church people, Lynn is wrong. The Bible does not deal with divorce and remarriage from Genesis to Revelation. The Bible, in fact, rarely deals with divorce and remarriage, and the Old Testament recognizes divorce as one of the facts of life among the Hebrews. Lynn and other churchmen need to examine the Scriptures, see exactly what it does say about divorce and remarriage, and interpret these passages in the light of the entire biblical picture.

Divorce first appears in the Old Testament in Deuteronomy 24:1–4. This passage does not institute divorce, but it does attempt to regulate it:

> When a man hath taken a wife, and married her, and it come to pass that she find no favour in his eyes, because he hath found some uncleanness in her: then let him write her a bill of divorcement, and give it in her hand, and send her out of his house. And when she is departed out of his house, she may go and be another man's wife. And if the latter husband hate her, and write her a bill of divorcement, and giveth it in her hand, and sendeth her out of his house; or if the latter husband die, which took her to be his wife; her former husband, which sent her away, may not take her

again to be his wife, after that she is defiled; for that is abomination before the Lord: and thou shalt not cause the land to sin, which the Lord thy God giveth thee for an inheritance.

Obviously divorce was just taken for granted by the Jews at this time. Moses and other leaders did not design any legislation to permit divorce or to justify it. Through this and other passages of Scripture they attempted to control this ageless custom. These verses do not prohibit divorce, nor pronounce any punishment upon the person being divorced, except in very specific cases, such as when a man seduces a young, unmarried woman (Deut. 22:28–29) or accuses his new wife of not being a virgin and is proved wrong (Deut. 22:13–19).

Deuteronomy recognizes remarriage as a natural result of the divorce, although this passage and others (Lev. 1:14; Jer. 3:1) warn against remarriage to the same man. Perhaps these restrictions about remarrying the former husband were designed to strengthen marriage and add finality to divorce. If a couple had a fight and in a fit of pique or anger went through with a divorce, they could not "make up" and remarry. The prohibition against remarrying the former husband did add the force of finality to the divorce procedure.

The Deuteronomy passage unfairly puts the initiative on the husband, a typical Old Testament family position. According to this passage, *if* (a conditional phrase) she loses favor in his sight (we would say they are incompatible), he may write a document that officially and legally frees her from the marriage.

Although the husband alone could determine the official grounds, we can be sure that the wife also had some role in the prelude to the divorce. Even in a society where polygamy was common and women were subjugated, there is evidence that women did indeed use their minds and wiles to get their way. We think of Sarah, Rebekah, Rachel, Michal, Bathsheba, and Delilah, not to mention the infamous Jezebel. I would suspect that many divorced women in the Old Testament did want the divorce for many of the same reasons that women want divorces today.

The Old Testament writers did not try to interpret or list the grounds for divorce. Jewish priests and interpreters, like their Christian counterparts today, tried to list grounds. The Jewish School of Hillel, for instance, ruled that if a woman burned her husband's bread, he had good reason for a divorce. Similarly, a preacher friend of mine counseled against divorce when a woman's legal husband had been missing for five years. My friend said that adultery, not absence, is the only biblical reason for divorce.

A rather long passage in Malachi 2 quotes God as saying, "I hate divorce":

And this have ye done again, covering the altar of the Lord with tears, with weeping, and with crying out, insomuch that he regardeth not the offering any more, or receiveth it with good will at your hand. Yet ye say, Wherefore? Because the Lord hath been witness between thee and the wife of thy youth, against whom thou hast dealt treacherously: yet is she thy companion, and the wife of thy covenant. And did not he make one? Yet had he the residue of the Spirit. And wherefore one? That he might seek a godly seed. Therefore take heed to your spirit, and let none deal treacherously against the wife of his youth. For the Lord, the God of Israel, saith that he hateth putting away: for one covereth violence with his garment, saith the Lord of hosts: therefore take heed to your spirit, that ye deal not treacherously (vv. 13–16).

This section may be one of numerous Old Testament passages in which the relationship of God and Israel is compared to marriage. This is one of the most frequent illustrations used by the Hebrew prophets. When Israel forsakes God and his law, it is referred to as unfaithful. These illustrations are summed up best in the Hosea-Gomer story. But if this Malachi quotation is not an illustration and is a literal treatment of divorce, it should be noted that God's desire out of the marriage is "godly offspring." This supports a popular religious view that the highest purpose of marriage is to produce children. If God does want children more than anything else out of a marriage, then it would follow that the ancient Hebrew practice of polygamy, especially in a childless marriage, would not only be acceptable, but would be pleasing to God.

The New Testament recognized the Hebrew divorce tradition but abolished it:

> The question was put to [Jesus]: 'Is it lawful for a man to divorce his wife?' This was to test him. He asked in return, 'What did Moses command you?' They answered, 'Moses permitted a man to divorce his wife by note of dismissal.' Jesus said to them, 'It was because you were so unteachable that he made this rule for you; but in the beginning, at the creation, God made them male and female. For this reason a man shall leave his father and mother, and be made one with his wife; and the two shall become one flesh. It follows that they are no longer two individuals: they are one flesh. What God has joined together, man must not separate.'

> When they were indoors again the disciples questioned him about this matter; he said to them, 'Whoever divorces his wife and marries another commits adultery against her: so too, if she divorces her husband and marries another, she commits adultery' (Mark 10:2–12, NEB).

There are parallel accounts in Matthew 19:1–12 and Luke 16:18. The Matthew account adds in verse 19, "Whoever divorces his wife, *except for unchastity*, and marries another, commits adultery." The same phrase, "except for unchastity," is also found in Matthew 5:32 in the Sermon on the Mount. Mark and Luke do not include the unchastity addition. Some scholars believe the Matthew addition is a late scribal entry and not what Jesus said.

It is clear at any rate that Jesus is setting a new standard against the Hebrew tradition that allowed a bill of divorce. This was not the first time that he had added to the law. His teaching was absolute. He explained to the Pharisees that Moses had allowed divorce because of closed minds. He also said that not everyone could accept his teaching (Matt. 19:11). Jesus always recognized the facts of sinful, incomplete, and failing men. This recognition of hard hearts and sinful weakness did not cause him to compromise his teachings or modify his ethics. He consistently proclaimed his ideals.

The question of divorce and remarriage was an issue among the early Christians. When it was raised in the Corinthian church, Paul followed Jesus in writing, "To the unmarried and to widows I say this: it is a good thing if they stay as I am myself; but if they cannot control themselves, they should marry. Better be married than burn with vain desire" (1 Cor. 7:8–9, NEB).

Paul went further by saying:

> To the rest I say this, as my own word, not as the Lord's: if a Christian has a heathen wife, and she is willing to live with him, he must not divorce her; and a woman who has a heathen husband willing to live with her must not divorce her husband. For the heathen husband now belongs to God through his Christian wife, and the heathen wife through her Christian husband. Otherwise your children would not belong to God, whereas in fact they do. If on the other hand the heathen partner wishes for a separation, let him have it. In such cases the Christian husband or wife is under no compulsion; but God's call is a call to live in peace. Think of it: as a wife you may be your husband's salvation; as a husband you may be your wife's salvation (1 Cor. 7:12–16, NEB).

Paul here introduces another exception to the absolute standards Jesus had given in Mark 10; according to this "Pauline privilege" a believer was free to divorce an unbeliever and to marry again, provided the next partner was also a believer.

It is interesting that in making this exception to the no-divorce rule, Paul does not refer to the "unchastity" exception in Matthew. Both of these exceptions have troubled the Church for centuries. If the Matthew passages are authentic, then how does one determine the unchastity of another? Is a man unfaithful to his wife only if he has sex with another woman? Or is he unfaithful if he lies and deceives? Did Jesus mean what he said when he taught that one committed adultery when one lusted (Matt. 5:27–28)? If so, then how is the husband or wife to really be sure that his or her mate has lusted? It is not difficult to decide that a man has been unfaithful to his wife when he moves in with another woman. But often adultery is denied. Is the churchman, or a marriage mate, supposed to hire a private eye to accumulate evidence of adultery? No one with any sense wants to play that game.

The Pauline exceptions have proven to be just as difficult. Paul knew what he meant by "believer," but no one since Paul has been that sure. Unfortunately, our world is filled with people who have been involved in one kind of religious persuasion or another, and who genuinely believe they are the "true believers." For centuries the Roman Catholic Church could not accept Protestants as "true believers," and the Protestants returned the insult. Some of the more dogmatic Fundamentalists and some of the more persuaded sects like Mormons, Adventists and Jehovah's Witnesses also have thought they have a corner on truth. In my own circle of friends, five couples have split up partly because of the "charismatic movement." The charismatic partner just can't tolerate the other's skepticism and "unbelief."

If unbelief is a valid reason for divorce, as the "Pauline privilege" suggests, then it is difficult to decide just what constitutes unbelief. And, as Paul hints, the believing husband or wife just might be able to win the unbeliever. Maybe they should wait and see.

We can maintain a strict and absolute interpretation

of the New Testament passages about divorce and remarriage. According to this absolute view, there is no room for divorce and no allowance for remarriage. The absolutist will not even attempt to handle the Matthean exception about unchastity or the Corinthian exception about unbelievers. The absolutist will not consider any of the other things that go wrong in marriage. He will say "One man, one woman, till death do us part" and that is it.

It seems to me that a person who interprets the divorce and remarriage passages that literally and absolutely will also have to interpret other New Testament passages literally and absolutely. To be literal, one should be consistent.

For instance, although the Church has been consistent in opposing divorce and remarriage, it has never been consistently opposed to war. Jesus said to love your enemies. Treat them well. Turn the other cheek. Give them your coat also. Resist not evil. He admonished Peter to put away his sword, saying that those who lived by the sword would die by the sword.

Rather than taking these clear teachings of Jesus and applying them rigidly, literally, and absolutely, the Church and most Christians have said that war is often justified. Our national wars have, until Viet Nam, been enthusiastically and prayerfully supported by the Church. Bible verses have been quoted, sermons preached and prayers said in support of the war effort.

When I was a boy growing up in a small county-seat town during World War II, I was impressed with the role of our church. Our pastor consistently prayed for victory. We saluted the flag. On Wednesday nights the pastor and relatives of servicemen read letters from the boys in Europe, the South Pacific and North Africa.

One man in our church declared himself a conscientious objector. This was a scandal to the church and the town. I still remember that people thought he was a coward. They shunned him. Although he claimed to be taking the Bible literally, no one respected him for that stance. That same church still would not allow a divorced man to be a deacon.

If the Church decided that tyranny is worse than war, the Church also decided that capital punishment was acceptable if it would decrease acts of violence and reduce crime. The Church has never been unanimous in opposing capital punishment. Christians have simply said that in a real world of crime and murder capital punishment, which is contrary to the teachings of Jesus, must be one of society's ways to control the criminal. One of my pastor friends, who will not marry anyone who is divorced, ran a full page message in a daily newspaper supporting the reinstitution of capital punishment (See Matt. 5: 38-39).

Most of us will take an oath as a witness (Matt. 5: 33-38). The Church does not judge or excommunicate the person who refuses to grant a loan or who refuses to give a coat to anyone who asks (Matt. 5:40-42). I do not know anyone who literally plucks out an eye or cuts off a hand (Matt. 5:29-30). Few Christians pray in closets (Matt. 6:6). Fasting is not a traditional religious exercise in most Protestant churches (Matt. 6:16). No one is advocating that a man be executed for murder if he hates his brother and no one says that the lustful look literally constitutes the act of adultery, although Jesus equates hate and murder, lust and adultery.

In spite of our accommodation of those other teachings of Jesus, we have, as churchmen, literally interpreted and enforced the ideals of Jesus regarding divorce and remarriage. We have universally disregarded some of the New Testament teachings and have said they cannot be applied literally in our world. Yet we have persistently said that the divorce and remarriage ideals can be applied literally.

At some point every Christian and every minister must make a decision about these Bible verses and his own life. I believe that "till death do us part" is the absolute

Bible teaching about marriage, divorce and remarriage. It is the ideal, the way God intended.

And there is a reason for the ideal of monogamy. Those of us who respect and honor the Bible believe that the laws of God have purpose. God does not dispense laws in an arbitrary way just to prove that he is God. He is not a strutting martinet who demands obedience to satisfy his ego. His commandments make sense. There is logic, especially in the historical setting, to his commandments.

The reason for monogamy in the Old Testament—and today—is to preserve the family unit. The family was, and is, the most basic relationship in society. Monogamy provides security and strength for every member of the family, and when a marriage breaks up the ramifications of that dissolution affect every member of the family.

The family unit is essential to the happiness and well-being of children. Monogamy gives the child security and substance. Little babies need constant care; they must be fed, changed, taught, and sheltered. They also need love, attention, and acceptance. They have emotional needs that must be supplied in those early years. They need their parents.

A child can be fed and housed and still deprived of warmth and love. A well-fed, physically-healthy child can grow into an immature, emotionally-sick adolescent if he is deprived of certain kinds of parental attention. The sick adolescent will become a miserable and dependent adult. Time after time these unhappy, disturbed adults will trace their problems back to their childhood. Often to a "broken home."

It seems obvious to me that monogamy was taught because it is best for the child. The child needs both mother and father for the proper balance in providing the physical and emotional needs. A human child leaves the nest slowly, and as life becomes more complex this preparation for leaving becomes more important.

Monogamy is also best for the man and woman involved. The husband and wife need one another. A couple is extremely fortunate when their marriage provides companionship and sharing. There are men and women who marry and who apparently never tire of the other's company. This is a beautiful, but rare, experience. It does happen—often enough to provide an inspiration for most newlyweds.

Husband and wife not only need companionship but they need the security, even the routine, that monogamy provides. This is represented by common ownership of property. A house to care for, to sleep and eat in, to pay for. A house to "come home" to. They need the roots and the belonging of monogamy. They need the feeling of being depended upon. Death or divorce creates complicated financial, property, and emotional problems for a husband or wife. More than tradition dictates that those kinds of settlements are made in courts with months of legal preparation. Monogamy packages up these complex family arrangements. When a marriage breaks up a Pandora's box of complicating factors is opened.

Our twentieth-century social structure is profoundly affected by the steady erosion of the family unit. As family solidarity decreases, society changes. This dissolution of the basic family unit produces more welfare payments, higher taxes, rising court costs, more juvenile delinquents, and numerous other social and governmental problems. The social fabric has been woven around the family unit. When this unit disintegrates our adjustment is clumsy and hesitant. It is hard to cope with broken families.

Monogamy is best. Divorce is always painful. Remarriage is always a risk. The Bible correctly condemns divorce and remarriage. But there are two Bible teachings that must be considered. The Bible teaches that God forgives and that we must forgive. God forgives divorce and remarriage too. The forgiveness principle is the great theme of the Bible. The theme of redemption, beginning again, is also a primary Biblical thrust. The ideals are clearly set out in the Scriptures, but when we fall short of the ideal, we can start over. Because love and marriage are so important, I think that especially the divorced person can start over. Or what is Christianity about?

I recognize and believe exactly what Jesus taught about the ideal of marriage. People can try to reach that ideal and fail. They can believe in monogamy and believe that divorce is wrong, and still be divorced. We all fail. We all fall short of the Biblical teachings about human behavior. God in his mercy and love forgives us when we fail. He constantly prods us by his spirit to "begin again." Remarriage is often a new beginning for his children.

# II.
# Handling
# Guilt

# "Some of my best friends
are divorced, but . . ."

"Sure, I know that people have been divorced ever since Old Testament times. Divorce is nothing new. I didn't invent it. It didn't begin with my divorce. It has always been around. And more people get divorces these days than ever before." Stanley is beginning one of those familiar conversations that divorced people conduct with their clergyman, with their friends and their relatives. Stanley is thinking about remarriage and he has to sort out his feelings about his own divorce before he can marry again.

"It's not that a divorcé is a freak. He doesn't belong in a side show. Everyone has friends and relatives who are divorced. Why," he smiled, "Some of my best friends are divorced.

"But it is different when you're the one. It's entirely different. I have told some of my friends who were thinking about remarriage to go ahead. No sweat. No problems. I wouldn't want to live alone, so if you want to marry again, do it. Some of them took my advice and they did marry again. Sometimes it has worked out, sometimes it hasn't. Anyway I gave them the advice to remarry casually; I didn't even think about their problems or their questions. Now that I'm trying to decide, there is a lot to consider."

Stanley is a successful businessman, the owner of three dry cleaner shops in our town. He has worked hard and made good money out of his business. He had been married about twenty years before his divorce and has two children in their late teens. Although most people were

33

surprised when Stanley and Carole were divorced, I had spent a lot of time with them and I wasn't surprised.

It had never been a good marriage to start with, and their relationship had deteriorated. They had gone through several years of emotional outbursts and sharp conflicts; then, after battling for several years they had both retreated into a kind of subtle nagging, followed by extended pouting periods when they simply did not communicate at all. This silence soon became a way of life that they tolerated. They each went their separate ways. They were courteous, but there was no communication and no caring. Eventually they both realized that there was just nothing between them. They simply did not care enough to try to put anything back together. They did not care enough to pout or to shout. It was all gone. What had been between them was fragile at best, and now there was nothing.

Stanley and Carole mutually agreed to the divorce. They did not argue about it. They discussed it calmly, reached certain decisions, and used the same attorney to get the legal work done. It all seemed perfectly calm and adult — two people who had been married for more than twenty years were legally affirming what had been an emotional fact for a long time. They no longer cared. They no longer wanted to live together. They did not want to be married.

Most of the friends and relatives who were surprised by the divorce were even more suprised by the calm attitude Stanley and Carole adopted. People couldn't quite believe that twenty years could be set aside so calmly and peacefully.

As it turned out, people were right. It is not that casual with Stanley. He has hang-ups about the divorce and remarriage. Stanley is not an active church man. He has always attended church services and has held some church assignments, but no one would call him "religious." Certainly no one would think his religion would bug him about anything. He isn't the type.

However, Stanley has been around the church long enough to absorb the position of the church about divorce and remarriage. No institution in our society has been as strong and forceful about divorce. The church's historical position has been incorporated into law in nearly every country and civilization where it has had influence. For three centuries divorce has been a moral, religious, and legal question in our nation, and only recently has the divorce question become a personal one between two adults in "no fault" divorce legislation. It is virtually impossible for a man like Stanley to ignore these three hundred years of moral, religious, and legal precedents.

More than that. Stanley has listened to his church all of his life. Not that he buys everything his church says—many of the church teachings Stanley accepts with a grain of salt. Although he does pray upon occasion, attends worship, professes to believe the Ten Commandments, gives money to the church, he has long since rejected the more revolutionary aspects of Christianity. But the church has done a good job on Stanley about divorce. He knows the church believes in "till death do us part." His parents, who had been married forty-three years when his father died, believed that, and Stanley knew that even if they had thought about divorce they wouldn't have gone through with it, because they thought divorce was wrong. Divorce went against God and the Bible, and Stan's parents weren't ever going to do anything they knew went against God and the Bible.

"Everything in the Bible speaks against divorce. One of my friends says that the Bible says God hates divorce and I guess he does. The same guy told me that Jesus said it was OK to get a divorce but that marrying again was a sin and if you had two living wives you were living in adultery. No one can be a Christian and live in adultery . . ."

Stan pauses and looks away out my window. "Maybe if divorce is a sin, you can get that sin forgiven. A lot of people get divorced and one or the other of them don't want it. God would know that and he surely wouldn't blame the one who didn't want the divorce. Of course, Carole and I are both guilty. We both wanted the divorce and we both agreed to it. So I guess we're both sinful about that. But when you get married again, that is a deliberate thing. You plan that new marriage. If it is a sin, it's one you sure plan on committing."

There is always some guilt associated with divorce. Religion has made divorce a moral question. The church has been uncompromising about divorce. I have found that morals and sin are not irrelevant and unimportant to people, especially people who have some kind of religious heritage. When a person has violated what he thinks is a moral law, he inevitably feels guilty. With this in his background, Stan and others like him will have to handle the question of guilt as he contemplates his remarriage.

One of the leaders in my church came to me and announced that he was going to divorce his wife. They had been married for six years. It was a second marriage for both of them. He said that he had been reading the Bible and that he knew they were living in adultery. He was not going to continue; he said he would rather be lonely the rest of his life than break the laws of God. I think he was sincere. He got the divorce and is still single. He was a very religious man who interpreted the Bible literally, but even a liberal Bible interpreter knows that the Bible categorizes divorce as a transgression of the plan of God. If a man or woman believes that divorce and remarriage are sinful and unforgivable, then they best not remarry. Any marriage will break under that kind of load of guilt.

Even if the couple do not divorce under the load of guilt, they will be doomed to years of anxiety and tension if they carry guilt into the new marriage. No one can be happy, open, and sharing if they think their relationship is illicit, immoral and indecent. Guilt will disturb any relationship. It is destructive; it breeds suspicion and distrust. Guilt brings depression and fear. It can corrupt and destroy the second marriage.

There are those people who seem to handle their guilt, who at least do not betray the symptoms of anxiety and suspicion that usually accompany guilt. But even some of these are convinced that God is angry with them and that he will surely "get them." They are waiting for the "other shoe to fall." Although they have remarried and the marriage is moving along smoothly, they secretly expect God to "get even." This surfaces as soon as some crisis or calamity comes to the marriage. At this point of suffering or trouble they say,"I expected this. God knew that we sinned when we married and he has just waited until now to bring his judgement upon us."

How can people handle their guilt feelings if they want to remarry? The Bible and the Church do indeed set out the ideal of monogamy until death do us part. This is an uncompromising position and it is the correct position. The stable family is not only a biblical ideal; it is a social necessity. We can expect the Bible to set out the correct ideals and we can expect the church to support these ideals. There are numerous Bible verses and two thousand years of church history to support monogamy.

There is also the biblical evidence that God is a merciful, loving Father who deals with us as persons, within or without our institutions. God is always at work caring for us and redeeming us individually. He may deal with nations, planets, or families but he certainly deals with persons. We may come to him corporately, but we certainly come to him individually. If God can love me as a person, then he must know and understand my personal needs, my personal gifts, and my personal sins.

There is no Biblical or historical evidence to suggest that divorce, or lust, or greed, or pride is unforgivable. There are no categories of sin. There are no good sins or bad sins. There is no way that God can be, on the one hand, the merciful Father that Jesus described and, on the other hand, an incensed tyrant who is waiting to do someone in because of a divorce or remarriage.

If you have some guilt feelings about remarriage that are based upon your religion, you might try to balance your guilt against the biblical and historical picture of the loving Father who knows all about us and understands, with mercy, our weaknesses and our strengths.

And remember the Genesis account of creation: it is not good that man should be alone. It wasn't good at the dawn of time and it isn't good today. The normal, natural state of love and companionship for man and woman is marriage. This was and is the plan of God. A divorce interrupts that, but it does not change it. Remarriage is an attempt to reconstruct what has always been a God-approved relationship between man and woman.

Sin? OK, so divorce and remarriage is sin. No one with religious sensitivity will treat sin casually. But no one will try to keep score either. No serious religionist will try to handle sin. It is too much. We can never measure up to the Biblical ideals. Love your enemies? Do good to people who use you? Quit lusting and coveting? Sell what you have and give it away? Love people like you love yourself? Don't let the sun go down on your anger? Think on things that are lovely? Pray without ceasing? Who are we kidding? There is no way that any of us can live up to it. No way that we can be perfect. There is too much humanity, too much weakness in us all.

I have long ago learned that the only way to handle my sin is to ask God in his mercy to love me. I have no doubt that he does. I really am not sure how he would feel about a new marriage, but that isn't a big problem. He loves me in spite of myself. He will always love me and will forgive my sin and my weakness. I'm counting on that. It is essential to my religion. It *is* my religion.

Not all guilt about divorce is related to religion. If the couple has had a lot of conflict prior to the divorce there will be some residual guilt that accumulates because of

things that were said and done during those times of conflict and controversy.

Stanley recalls reluctantly some of that acrimony.
"Well, it's not only the religious thing. I feel real bad
about a lot of the fighting that Carole and I did. By the
time we decided to get the divorce, we had quit that
stuff. But we sure had some bad fights.

"It's not what the kids heard, although they heard too
much. They probably heard us say things they will never
forget. But it's not the kids; it's some of the things we
said to one another. It really can be rough in that kind of
marriage. I have said things to Carole that I have never
said to anyone else. You just get so frustrated and fed up
in an unhappy marriage, and in anger all of that ugly talk
comes out. It's strange, but I still remember some of
those verbal fights.

"We finally quit fighting. We practically quit talking
before we got the divorce. I'm not thinking much about
those years of silence, but it seems like I relive those bad
fights and I still remember the things we said. I don't
know whether we meant them or not. I really don't know
why we said those things. But we said them to hurt one
another and they did hurt.

"Now I'm having a problem with that. Maybe there is
some way that I can talk to Carole and apologize. Gee, I
didn't mean to hurt her and I don't think she aimed to
hurt me. All of that bad talk is still with me, though.

"You know when you're into that, you say cruel things.
Like you pick out things that will embarrass or humili-
ate. You say nasty things about the way a person looks or
something else that they can't help. When you get sore
like that you insult a person. Or you make a lot of accu-
sations that you know aren't true. You accuse the other
one of being dishonest, or a fake, or unfaithful. You say
things about their motives or their behavior. Or about
their sincerity. Now as I look back at some of those
fights, I feel guilty as hell."

Stanley may be able to talk this particular guilt over

with Carole and they might be able to forgive the ugly and angry fights that preceded the divorce. But in many cases this kind of fence-mending is unwise and unnecessary. Most marriage fights are eventually ended in divorce; they are just part of the residue of the broken marriage that must be put aside.

Stanley can feel guilt about the fighting if he wants to, but there is very little he can do about it. The fighting was not a cause of the divorce, but was a symptom of the basic conflict in the marriage. The events that provoked the fights should have been handled differently, but the fights were decisive in breaking up the marriage. I suspect that Stanley is wanting Carole's forgiveness, not so much to ease his guilt about the fights, but to get some assurance about his new marriage. He is afraid that this same kind of infighting might reappear.

How can we handle this guilt about the things that were said prior to or during the divorce? We can remember that the conflict was an accumulation of frustration and disappointments. There was no good communication and sharp vituperation was the poor substitute. The anger was not unilateral, and both parties said and did things that hurt the other. Pain was intentionally inflicted and that is not a pleasant thought. But it has happened and it is past. It is not necessarily going to be repeated in another marriage. It is not necessarily a personality trait that will reappear. It is not the best way to handle frustration; it is not the only way to deal with conflict. Hopefully, the divorced person has learned enough from experience not to repeat it.

Guilt is a strange phenomenon. It is most often encouraged by the guilty person. It can become an obsession that drives us into depression and other forms of mental and emotional illness. It can become a way to gain attention and sympathy from people who do not pay us enough attention. It can be a way for us to get acceptance from others when we have strong feelings of inadequacy and unimportance.

To be sure, there are always those people around who try to make us feel guilty. They will exploit guilt for financial gain, or for personal power, or just because they are mean and get their kicks that way. But the exploiters must find willing subjects, and there are always people who want to be spanked because they feel guilty or think they should feel guilty.

Stanley can live without his guilt and can find a happy, useful life if he will let God be his loving Father and if he will let the past be the past with Carole. "Having put his hand to the plough, he need not look back."

# "What about the children?"

"I would have left Elaine a dozen years ago if it hadn't been for the children. Finally, when I couldn't stand it anymore, I filed for divorce. I have no problem about Elaine. I don't love her. I never loved her. It was a rotten marriage. But the thing with the children still tears me up. Now that I'm about to marry again, the situation is worse."

Carl is an emotional man. He wears his feelings openly and expresses them freely. I know Carl and I know people like Carl. They feel intensely. They do not wear masks. They have integrity and they are not ashamed of their feelings. He is telling me now about something that is vitally and essentially important. He is talking about his children and Carl's children are important to him.

When Carl and Elaine were divorced the children were the most important consideration to both of them. Their children are about six, nine, and twelve. None of them is teenage. All of them love their Daddy and they love their Mother. Elaine is more reserved than Carl. She is not as open or as emotional, but she is good to the children. There was no controversy about custody. They both agreed that Elaine would have custody and Carl would visit often, which he has. There were no problems about finances; Carl always paid more than the child support order called for. As much as possible they had worked this out agreeably.

The agreeability has helped Carl with his guilt, but it hasn't eliminated it. Carl thinks he should be at home with the children like his father was with him. He is not comfortable "visiting" his children.

"I have never felt right about it. I should be there when they bring in report cards, or when the dog is sick, or to put them to bed at night. I should be there at breakfast, or when they just want to talk. Sure, I'm around more than most divorced fathers, but it just isn't the same.

"Now that I'm going to marry again, that will change. I can't be around the kids and my ex-wife that much. It wouldn't be fair to my new wife. And let's face it, I'm in love with the woman I'm going to marry and I don't want to leave her to go to the old house. The kids and I are going to drift apart."

Carl is right. He is right on all counts. The divorce has been painful to the children. They have missed him and they do not understand why he left. No one can correctly assess or analyze how children react to a divorce. It depends upon the child and the conditions of the marriage prior to the divorce. Two children will react differently to the same divorce. It is certain that a divorce is traumatic to any child and that adjustment takes time.

When Carl moved out, things essentially changed for Elaine and the three children. Nothing was the same at that house. Things also changed for Carl. The situation will never be like it was before his move. As their circumstances changed, all of the people in that family changed and none of them are today what they were the day Carl left the family. It is impossible for any of them to reconstruct the family that was before the divorce.

It is important that Carl, Elaine, and the children understand that. I think children understand and accept that fact better than the parents. Children miss the absent parent. They may try to scheme him back home. They may cry at night. They may be angry with the parent that stays at home. They may exploit the other parent. They may feel neglected and odd in their new status, but I think they know that something has happened and that it will never be the same.

Carl will have to accept the fact that he has changed

his relationship with his children. He has changed it, but not necessarily destroyed it. If he will, he can build some new kinds of experiences with his children. This will require some thought and planning. It will not be accidental or natural. He must try to establish times, places and ways to keep close to them. This will be important to his future happiness and to theirs.

This kind of planning will consider his new life with his new wife. They should discuss his children and his plans for his children in their premarital conversation. He must tell her that he plans to keep in touch with his children, that he plans to do things with them and for them, and that he plans to keep a relationship. This is not at the expense of the new marriage, but it is part of his life.

Carl knows his new wife may see the children as rivals for his affection, his time, and his money. Carl has spent a lot of time with his children. He is right. When he marries again he will not want to spend that much time away from his new wife. Things will be different.

There are understandable reasons for his guilt about his children; he not only has left them, but he has hurt them. Most small children interpret a divorce personally. They do not know what has gone on between the parents; they only know what goes on between the parent and child. When the parent leaves home, the parent leaves the child.

Carl has read articles and stories about children from broken homes. Before his divorce, he pitied children from one-parent families. Now his own children are thrust into that category, and he feels it is his fault. This is uncomfortable and produces guilt.

At times Carl contemplates asking Elaine for a reconciliation for the sake of the children. For years he and Elaine had sustained their marriage for the sake of the children. Finally they had decided that the children were not reason enough. They had decided that there was more to marriage, more to life, than maintaining a marriage just so that their children would have two parents. This had been a deliberate decision that they had talked about over the years. They both thought that they had looked at the matter carefully and made the best decision.

Apparently Elaine has adjusted to it. But she is living with the children. Carl is having more difficulty because he does not see the children as often as Elaine does. And Carl feels like the children feel differently about him than before. He thinks he picks up things in their countenance and their conversation. At times when he is alone Carl is nearly overwhelmed with guilt because he has hurt his children.

"Any man who hurts a child is a tramp. But when a man hurts his own children, children that he says he loves, that man is wrong. He is really wrong!"

Like all divorced people with young children, Carl also tries to cope with the idea that someone else may rear his children. Elaine will probably marry again. If she does, his children will have a new father. A stepfather. Another man will help them with their home work; another man will send them off on their first date; another man will go with them to the dentist. Eventually that other man will take Carl's place with the children just as he has taken Carl's place with Elaine.

"I brought them into the world. I remember like it was yesterday, the day each one of them was born. It was a great feeling! Like every parent, I've tried to see something of myself in each one of these kids. And it's there. Each one of them has some of my traits, some of my characteristics. They didn't ask to be brought into the world, but we brought them. Now I've left them. Someone else will be rearing them. Someone else, someone I don't even know, will be taking my place with my kids.

"On the other hand, the divorce is over. Elaine and I just could not work out our problems. It was a rotten marriage. We were both miserable and unhappy. The kids knew about a lot of the conflict, but there were things wrong in that marriage that no one knew, things that we couldn't describe. It was no good. It is over and I know that it was right and best to divorce. I am positive about my plans to marry again. I will be happy. This is not a sudden decision; we have been together a lot and we are sure this is right. Can the divorce be right, the new marriage be right, and my feelings about the children be wrong? How can I put all of this together?"

Carl is facing up to the complex emotional pain of divorce and remarriage. The children are in the center of his confusion. This has been his thought pattern for years. By his own admission the children had kept him and Elaine together after they both knew that their marriage was a failure. His life has been pointed toward his children. They have been the objects of his love; he has not loved Elaine. They have given him love; Elaine has not loved him. He has been interested in their daily activities. He has shared their joys and their frustrations.

Carl has had some success in his work, and he has said that he worked hard for his children. He wanted to get ahead in his work so that his children could have more things—things he did not have as a boy. He has tried to succeed and hoped that the children would enjoy his successes, that they would be proud of him. Elaine has been disinterested in Carl's work and he has tried to find approval and love from his children.

These kinds of things have been more important to Carl than to his children. He has exaggerated this parental role of his. The kids have not been impressed with the things he buys. They have assumed that the "things" were part of their family. They can get along on less, or if there were more things, they would not be more impressed. They are also relatively unaware of his successes. They know where he works and what he does. They are not capable of sharing his prestige and his status. This is not important to them.

I have a friend who is a university teacher. When his former wife married a bus driver and the bus driver became the resident father of his children, he moaned for weeks about "what this unfortunate marriage would do to my children." The children were actually indifferent to bus driving or university teaching. They are much more interested in what kind of man is filling the parental role than in what he does.

Can Carl handle his guilt feelings about the children? I don't know. His relationship with his children is unalterably changed. They have been hurt and they will forever feel differently about him. He has lost some things that are important to children and important to parents. There is some finality to this change.

But our relationship with our children is always changing. It *should* be changing. Healthy families understand and encourage the change. As children get older, it is essential that they become more independent and more free from parental influence. Apron strings must be cut. This is always difficult for parents and it is always desirable.

Carl has left his children before they are teens, but in a few short years there would be a "leaving" anyway. They will grow into a more independent life style. They will be less dependent upon him. They will isolate themselves more from him; they will rebel against his authority and resent his interference in their lives. Passing time will eventually change his relationship with his children.

He has rushed that inevitable process by his divorce and remarriage. He has probably forced his children into independence at an earlier age, but it was going to happen sometime. Some children move toward maturity more quickly than others, but they all come to some declaration of independence.

I have already suggested that Carl can try to rearrange and reorder his relationship with the children. He should make plans with his new wife to include his children in his new life at appropriate times and in appropriate ways. He cannot resume the relationship he had with the children prior to, or even after, the divorce. But he can make some new kinds of relationships.

There is no way that Carl can change the past. He can

brood about it, analyze it, or castigate himself. He can indulge his guilt and become morose and melancholy. He can feel sorry for himself and for the children. But none of this will change anything. Wisely or foolishly, Carl decided to get a divorce. It cannot be changed. The family that once was is forever gone. But that family was constantly changing anyway. Every day meant change. There was no way that Carl could have preserved the family as he knew it. The divorce was a dramatic fracture in that family, but there were other things operating all of the time that were bringing changes to his family.

It is important, as Carl plans to marry again, that he realize the past is past. He cannot reconstruct his relationship with his children. He can, however, develop new relationships with his children that will bring something to their life and will give him some sense of parenthood.

All is not lost; it is just different.

# "I have failed"

"You can put any name on it you want to, but a divorce is a failure. No one ever gets married and expects to get a divorce. They all think it will work out. Sure, they know that divorce statistics are high and rising all of the time. Every newly-married couple knows people who have avoided divorce, but have been unhappy in marriage. Really unhappy. Even with these facts, they all think their marriage is going to be happy. Nothing is going to break them up. I thought that. I was convinced of it. I thought anyone who really wanted to could make a marriage work. But I failed."

Jayne has not failed often in her life, but she did fail in her first marriage. Now that she is ready to marry again, that first failure sticks with her and makes her uncomfortable and unsure about remarrying. Jayne must cope with that failure before she begins a new marriage.

"I thought I was sure the first time. I was not a starry-eyed kid. Dan and I met in college. We were both mature for our age. We had been in love before and this was not a first-time affair. We dated for ten months. Steady. We were together all of the time and we knew one another. At least we thought we knew one another. We talked a lot. We thought we had a good time. There was sex appeal. At least we thought all of these things were operating.

"Our lives had some similarity. We had grown up in the same kinds of families. Incidentally, we got along real well with the in-laws—that is, until we began having trouble and the in-laws took sides. The in-laws eventually helped break us up, but at first we had so much in common. It seemed that we could just pick up our lives and go right on together in happiness and compatibility. Our marriage was the kind that people approved of.

"When the marriage began to unwind, we were both concerned. We were surprised. We thought that we could handle it. We were rational, intelligent people who could handle anything. We both thought that we could work it out, talk it out, put it together. So we had endless hours of conversation. When these sessions didn't help, we went to a counselor. We were both willing to be counseled. We tried to cooperate.

"But nothing worked. Everything we did backfired. We became more impatient, more separated, and finally more hostile. We went through all the forms and carried out the suggestions. But all the time we were trying to put it together with Band-Aids and string, the thing was coming apart in the middle. I don't know how to explain any of it, except to say that we really didn't care at all about each other. All of our patching was a game. We were trying to do something that neither one of us felt. It was terrible! Our mistake was in getting married and I will never understand why we married in the first place."

Jayne is genuinely perplexed. She does not know why she married Dan and she still wonders about it. This bad marriage and subsequent divorce has damaged her ego and her self esteem. She made an error in judgement and Jayne has privately had a lot of confidence in her own judgement. She failed to make the right marriage choice and this has damaged her self-confidence. She not only is embarrassed by this bad decision, but she feels guilty about the failure to preserve the marriage.

She is the kind of person who believes that everything can be worked out satisfactorily if a person tries. Jayne always looks for answers and has been successful in finding answers. When someone has a setback, Jayne assumes that he or she did not try hard enough to succeed. When someone faces an obstacle, Jayne believes the obstacle can be overcome with ingenuity and persistence.

Like many people, she is success-oriented. From early childhood, she had been taught to succeed. Her parents wanted her to be popular, to make good grades in school, and to gain recognition in her community. In college she followed this same path to achievement and awards. After her marriage she chose certain roles in her church and community. She was an achiever in these roles and developed a deserved reputation as one who could get things done.

Now one of the basic relationships in her life had broken to pieces and she couldn't fix it. Part of her role and image was dependent upon her status as Dan's wife. Her image was changed by the divorce. This failure was bitter and distasteful.

Other people less self-confident than Jayne have felt that failure, too. At any level of esteem, a divorce is a blow to the ego. It takes time to get this feeling into focus. There is normally a progression of emotional reactions.

The first question born in the guilt of failure relates to the reasons for the first marriage, and those reasons are accented when you contemplate the next marriage. If I used poor judgement and made a bad marriage the first time, how can I be sure my judgement has improved? Will I make another bad choice? Maybe I'm just not able to judge the marriage potential of a person.

Unfortunately some people do make the same mistake in marriage twice. They will choose a person for the next marriage who is similar to the person they divorced. They probably do this because they are more comfortable with that kind of person, even if the other marriage failed.

No one is all bad. The former mate did have some good and attractive qualities. It might be smart to get these good qualities in your mind. The things that you enjoyed the most in your former mate can be found in others. The character qualities you admired the most can be found in others. By contrast, you should be aware of the things in your former mate that turned you off and eventually ruined the marriage. You did not change those disagreeable traits in the first partner and you will not change them in a new candidate for marriage. Do not repeat your errors of the past.

Any mature person learns from the past and especially from the mistakes of the past. This is very important as you plan another marriage. It should mean that you have learned from the mistakes of the past.

Part of the guilt of failure comes when you begin to rehearse the events that led up to the divorce. The divorcee always wonders, "What could I have done to save the marriage? I know that I should have tried harder. We should have been more willing to compromise. We should have gone to a counselor. We should have been less rigid and stubborn. This marriage would have lasted, if we had just worked at it more than we did."

When a person relives a failure, he or she normally recalls certain crisis situations that seem to be turning points. In hindsight we can see the errors made during those crisis times. This is at least partially true. There are certain crisis times in every experience and a failing marriage is no exception. If that crisis had been handled differently, things might have been different.

The crisis might have been the birth of a child. Or the annual vacation. Or a job change. Or a visit to the in-laws. The crisis might have been a suspected extramarital affair or the purchase of a home. The crisis might have been precipitated by a clash with an in-law or an unexpected financial setback. In retrospect the crisis does not seem important, but it was important at the time. Divorced people look back at the crisis and wonder how it could have caused so much trouble.

Kirt and Sharon had a continuing conflict about his work and her parents. Kirt was involved in various community projects and was active in his church. He was self-employed and spent too many hours at work. Sharon's parents were older and they lived out of town.

Sharon was devoted to her parents and was dependent upon them. She wanted Kirt to go with her often to visit her parents. She wanted to spend most weekends with her parents and her friends in the parents' town.

They had tried to work this problem out. Kirt had encouraged her to visit her parents while he was at work. At times he would agree to go with her for a weekend. But their attempts at solving the problem did not work out. The tension grew and the crisis came when Sharon's mother had surgery. Sharon went to stay with her father. Kirt agreed. Then when her mother came home from the hospital, Sharon decided to stay longer. They had a serious fight about it over the phone. Kirt was busy for two days and did not call Sharon back for an apology or any form of reconciliation. This was their crisis.

They both refer to the crisis over her mother's surgery as the "straw that broke the camel's back." They both feel guilty. They think they should have worked out the problem about the mother's surgery. Of course their problems were not that superficial. Sharon had never been willing to leave her parents and her small-town friends. Kirt had not been willing to give Sharon any priority on his schedule. He was absorbed with his career, his reputation, and his activities.

Now they exaggerate the crisis. They may be oblivious to the real problems in their relationship. Or they may be aware of them, but they are still not capable of dealing with these problems honestly. In either case, they both say that the marriage failed because they did not handle the crisis properly. They feel guilty because of this failure in crisis.

"I could have quit drinking. She was always nagging me about booze and she kept saying I couldn't quit. She was always saying I was becoming an alcoholic. But that wasn't true; I just enjoyed a drink. And I never told her I would quit drinking if she married me. Why, even if there was a drinking problem, there are ways to get help. I know a fellow at work who goes to A.A. and he hasn't had a drink in two years. I would have tried to get help if I'd known it was that important to her. I feel badly that we let something like booze break us up."

"I know that I talked a lot about my boss. My husband, my ex-husband that is, had wanted me to work. There aren't many jobs around for women that don't include some men workers too. My husband was always jealous. He never trusted me. But I didn't realize that he was so jealous of my boss. When I came home from work and tried to tell him about my day, I just naturally talked about my boss. I just didn't realize it was getting to him. Then he came bursting in on my boss and me that night in a restaurant. You would have thought we were in a hotel room and all we were doing was eating dinner together. It was a bad scene. But if I'd known that it would lead to divorce, I could have changed jobs to save my marriage. It's too late now."

"My wife kept saying that we should talk to our pastor about our marriage. I didn't want to talk to anyone about it. Marriage should be private and personal. Who wants to go tell someone all of the intimate things about their marriage? I knew the pastor and he is OK. He has some experience talking to people who have marriage problems, but I figure that everyone who is married has problems. At least everyone I know has problems. I didn't think ours were any different. Our marriage was no worse, no better, than others. But I was sure wrong. She went right on with a divorce, then told me that I could have helped save it if we had gotten some counseling. After she filed for divorce I went to the pastor, but it was too late. I don't know why I didn't go when she wanted me to."

In each case the person has guilt because of the failure of the former marriage. In most cases the guilt is not justified because it is based upon a shallow assumption. To be sure, a marriage must be worked out. But the work must be done in the areas of conflict. Too much "work" is done dealing with the symptoms or the expressions of the problem, rather than dealing with the roots of the problem.

Everyone who has been divorced can recall failures. The events leading up to the divorce may be an accumulation of failures. A person may have been insensitive to the feelings of their partner. They may have been inclined to exaggerate or minimize the conflicts. There may have been times and places that could have been changed. They both may have been stubborn. This accumulation of failures eventually produced the divorce, and the divorce is a failure.

If a person is going to marry again, what can he or she do about those failures? It is important to try, as much as possible, to sort them out objectively and gain some knowledge from the experience. Failure is not final. One failure does not mean a succession of failures. No one is a born loser.

To feel guilty about those failures is an exercise in self-pity. Admitting the failure and acknowledging the mistakes is the first step on the road to recovery. There is no need to rehearse the failures, to keep talking about them, to punish yourself. The divorce is the punishment and the result of the failure. It is time now to get out of the past. The divorced person needs to look ahead, determine not to repeat the same mistakes and not to dwell upon them. It is time to put failure behind.

On entering their new marriage, divorced people should have an advantage. They know now where they are vulnerable and weak. They know some things about marriage that are destructive and serious. They also know some things that work. Things about marriage that bring happiness. The past is behind the divorced person. It is important to leave it there.

# III.
# Lifestyle
# Changes

# "I was familiar with Vicki's lifestyle"

"My first marriage was not happy. We had all kinds of disagreements and conflicts. We fussed and pouted. We screamed and yelled. We went our separate ways. But we did live together for nine years, and during nine years there are certain things that you get used to in a husband or wife. There are some predictable parts of a marriage. You learn how your mate is going to act. When you think about a new marriage, you realize that your new mate is not going to be like the last one."

Don is an engineer who works for a large local company. He has been divorced for ten months and he is thinking about remarriage. He has been dating one of the women he works with. They have seriously discussed marriage and Don is trying to sort out his feelings about a second marriage.

"I do not have a lot of guilt about my divorce from Vicki. We just had a bad marriage and our divorce did not produce hostility. We have both agreed that the nine years was a fair trial. It just didn't work. We are grateful that there were no children to complicate everything. When we got the divorce we thought we could both start all over and there was still time for us to find happiness.

"After living alone in an apartment for ten months, I've realized that the nine years with Vicki have had a profound influence on my life. It makes me nervous about marrying someone else, even a woman I love. And I do love Gail. We both believe that we can be happy, or we wouldn't even contemplate marriage. We are adults.

"But there are so many things about a former husband

**61**

or wife that stick with you. I know how Vicki cleared her throat and what those sounds mean. Do you learn those throat-clearing sounds from a new wife? I know what Vicki liked to eat for breakfast; I know how long it took her to fix her hair before we went to church. I know what T.V. program she likes; I know how she cleans up the house; I know her mannerisms. I know what she laughs about, what makes her angry, and I could anticipate her tears.

"I don't think this familiarity is to be confused with love. It certainly is not the same as compatibility or happiness in marriage. Perhaps a man can be that familiar with his secretary, or his working associates. He is surely that familiar with his parents, his brothers and sisters at home. At the same time there is some hesitancy about entering into another marriage with a new partner with whom you are not familiar. Familiarity may breed contempt, but familiarity in my case is comfortable.

"Maybe I'm shy. I think a lot of people are shy about something as intimate as marriage. Even the loud, self-confident, extroverted type of person is probably shy about the intimacies of a marriage. So a shy person moves very gingerly and cautiously into a marriage. He is self-conscious and careful. He doesn't want to be embarrassed at any point in the early days of the marriage. Those early days of the marriage involve a lot of careful experimentation, not just about sex either.

"All of that takes a while. But eventually you get some comfort. You are not self-conscious about your growling stomach, or your bad teeth, or your penchant for peanut butter and bananas. Your wife knows how you look and act when you have a cold or when you have diarrhea. She knows that you like to read "Dear Abby" and that you scratch your left ear when you're under pressure. She learns that you drum your fingers when you're bored and lick your lips when you're angry. She knows by the sound of your voice what is coming next. She knows what kind of underwear you prefer and that you don't feel right about the way your Dad wrote his will. Everything she knows about you, you know comparable things about her."

Don is talking about one of the important questions to be faced in a new marriage. Although the first marriage did not work, there was a certain kind of familiarity that grew in that first marriage. This familiarity is one of the things that keeps marriages together. Many people who discuss divorce are reluctant to go the divorce route because they do not want to trade off a familiar relationship for one that is unfamiliar. They discuss divorce, but decide that it is not worth the risk. They prefer to stay with what they know.

There is a kind of routine in every relationship. It takes a while to establish that routine, but after the routine is discovered most married couples fall into it. Disrupting the routine and changing a familiar lifestyle is often one of the primary causes of pre-divorce hassling. When the marriage routine is developed, any deviation in an inflexible marriage is interpreted as a serious breach of contract. One of the things most people look for in marriage is predictability and routine. They want the stability and dependability that the routine provides.

If this routine is violated, the other partner may panic. This idea carries over when a new marriage is contemplated. What kind of routine can you work out with a new mate? How will this routine compare with the schedule that you were accustomed to and comfortable with in the former marriage?

Don continues, "Let me tell you some things that I'm thinking about. Vicki always got up early in the morning. I like to sleep late, but she would get up, read the paper, fix breakfast and be wide awake when she woke me. Gail likes to sleep like I do. Maybe it's silly when you're in love, but will Gail get me up? She says she will, but I know she hates to get up even more than I do. And for nine years I've been sleeping late waiting for my wife to get me up.

"Vicki wasn't much on keeping house. In fact our house was messy. At times I was embarassed to have guests in. So I got in the habit of doing some of the housework. And I did some griping to Vicki about the house. Now Gail is a very clean person, but she does it her own way. In fact she is so particular about things that we will have some problems about that. Vicki ate every meal at a certain time. She didn't like to cook, but she was always determined to eat at a certain time. Gail doesn't want to eat until she is hungry. I have gotten used to eating at certain times. I know that these things don't sound important, but they can be."

There are many personal adjustments to make in any marriage. The second marriage requires an entirely new set of adjustments. When you marry the first time you must adjust from a single life to a sharing life with another person. This is always difficult and takes time. Remarriage not only means adjustment, but you must set aside the familiar lifestyle of the former marriage.

Although there are some similarities in any marriage by the same person that are dictated by house, job, children, and recreation, there are also certain changes that will take place in the new marriage. These changes may be obvious or subtle, but they must be encountered and dealt with. The marriage license will not eliminate them.

Barbara divorced her husband because she had gotten into a love affair with a man that she worked with. The affair had lasted more than one year and she felt that she was ready for remarriage when her divorce was granted. Barbara had been married five years and she did not have any children. Her former husband was not really surprised when Barbara announced the divorce. He had known their marriage was shaky. Although he was not surprised, he was disappointed. He was not acrimonious and he did not lose his temper with Barbara. She was the dominant partner and she was accustomed to making decisions that her husband accepted. She always had an air of self-confidence.

"My divorce is right. The marriage was poor and I'm sure that I love Gary. We have been together nearly every day for a year. We are both mature people and we are not jumping into anything," Barbara said.

"Even with those facts—the bad marriage and the love affair—I'm worried about the changes a new marriage will bring. I know that marriage to Gary means a new set of friends. My former husband and I had a set of friends that I can no longer enjoy. Some friends are embarrassed by the divorce. They think they have to take sides. They are uncomfortable. Consequently we will give up that set of friends. Some of our friends are already gone because of the divorce; another marriage will blow their minds. Not that they are necessarily judgmental, but that's just the way it works out.

"And Gary will expect me to feel comfortable with his personal friends and business associates. I won't feel comfortable with them and I dread the times when I must be introduced to them.

"Most of us are creatures of habit. I am anxious about learning his habits. I want to please him. I want to make him happy. But he has certain habits and routines that are not familiar to me. There are little things that I will not catch or pick up on. Little things in his home that are important to him. If this was a first marriage we could learn together, but in a second marriage, we must unlearn before we can relearn. That frightens me.

"No man is like the man I was married to the first time. Of course there were many things about my first husband that I didn't like, or I wouldn't have divorced him. But I did know him. I did know what to expect. Now I have to learn again what really turns a different man on and what really turns him off. This can be frightening!"

A new marriage usually means a new house or apartment. Americans are transient and very few live in the same house very long. A generation ago it was normal for a married couple to live a lifetime in one house. They were usually surrounded by relatives and it was not uncommon for one family to own a house or land for a century or more. Our urban culture has changed that.

But even transient people must adjust to the new physical and geographical setting that divorce and remarriage bring. A new place to live, a new section of town, a new city, or a new state may be the result of a new marriage.

The new marriage will also change the finances in the new family. No two couples will budget and spend money the same way. Remarriage may mean a drastic kind of financial adjustment. Money will be important in the next marriage, perhaps more important than in the first one.

Barbara is aware of this: "In my first marriage I managed the money. My husband and I both worked and earned middle income salaries. We deposited our checks and I paid the bills. He did not worry about finances. His tastes were simple and modest. He was not ambitious for money or status. I do enjoy money and the things money can buy. We did not quarrel about finances, but I managed all of the money.

"Gary earns more money than my former husband. A lot more money. Gary likes money and he spends money. I have privately wondered about the way he handles money and have a suspicion that he is extravagant and may overspend. He likes to impress people with his spending. I have been accustomed to modest spending and this could be a problem. Gary and I do not look at money the same way, but I know that no two people would have the same familiar values about money that were evident in a previous marriage."

Barbara is right. In the area of finance, as well as other aspects of married life, there must be some unlearning and some relearning. The new family must make all of the adjustments that were necessary in the first marriage. This is not insurmountable, but it should be expected.

A person who goes into a new marriage, must be willing to accept a new routine, new habits, and a new family lifestyle. The next marriage will not be like the previous marriage. There will be changes. Some of these changes will be welcome; some will be surprising; others will be embarrassing and unfamiliar. If a couple cannot be flexible, they should rethink their plans for a new marriage. If they are willing to adjust to change, they can work out a new routine in their new family.

A new routine is not a moral question, not a question of right or wrong. Most routines develop because they are comfortable and mutually acceptable. This acceptability can give the routine an aura of sanctity, but this is a confused judgment. Routines *can* be changed without reflecting on anyone's good sense or personal worth. Every family soon develops habits merely by repetition. When those habits are never challenged and never changed, they become too important. Do not give the routines too much value; keep a proper perspective about the important things in the marriage. A new marriage can transcend the problems of adjustment if both partners remain flexible.

## "There is so much to adjust to"

Everyone who marries again has a new family. There is a new husband or wife, new in-laws, and new relationships with your own family. Even when family members say they "are not very close," there is always some mysterious bridge between them. The introduction of a new family member is always an important event and is approached with hesitancy.

"I am ready to marry Ralph," Judy told me. "We are engaged and have made wedding plans. There is still one problem, though. I must take Ralph to my home in Indiana to meet my family. I haven't lived at home for fourteen years, counting college, but I am reasonably close to my family at home. Mother and Dad are still living, and I have two married sisters in that town, plus two grandmothers. All of them took my divorce hard. They were not that impressed with my first husband, but they did like him. They all feel strongly against divorce. They will not approve of another marriage.

"Mother did an entire grief scene when I went home to tell them I was getting a divorce. She went to bed with a sick headache, said that I had disgraced the family, had disobeyed the laws of God and all of the rest. It was really a bad scene. She overreacted so much that Dad kind of took my side. Not that Dad approved. He never said that he approved. But he was at least kind to me and I have never felt that he turned on me. I know that Mother will do the scene again. I'm not sure about Dad.

"Ralph complicates the problem for me. He is not much like my former husband. My ex went out of his

**69**

way to please Mother and Dad. Ralph won't do that. In fact, if they throw a fit Ralph will fight back at them. He is already down on them from what I've said. My attitude has made him defensive and suspicious of my parents. I should have been more careful.

"Although I love and respect my parents, I am used to being in conflict with them. I can handle that. I have to live my own life and I have the right to marry Ralph and be happy with him. I would like to have my parents' approval, but don't expect it. This doesn't worry me that much. I left home years ago, and I know that my relationship with them is constantly changing. A new marriage is just another way that it changes. Even Jesus said that you leave your mother and father and cleave to one another. My parents are not that important in my new marriage.

"I do have a problem with Dad's mother. She is my favorite grandmother—I guess she is my favorite relative. My memories of childhood always include her. I remember eating at her house every Sunday at noon. I remember staying all night at her house every Thursday night of my childhood. When I left home for college and went through the homesick times, it was always my grandmother that I thought about.

"She did not say much about the divorce, but she was hurt. She looked old and in pain when I told her about the divorce. When I finished explaining it, she kissed me and told me she hoped I would be happy.

"She is a very religious person. Old country church religion. She and Grandpa were married fifty-one years when he died. He was hard to like. He must have tried her patience and her love a million times, but they stayed married fifty-one years. She probably thought of divorce and immediately rejected it. Anyone who lived with Grandpa would have thought of divorce.

"I know that Grandma will not want me to marry Ralph, or anyone. She will think that remarriage is wrong. I do not want to face Grandma. No matter what is said and no matter what she thinks of Ralph, things will change between Grandma and me.

"My sisters and I are not that close. I am not really concerned about their opinions. It would be nice if they approved, but their attitude does not affect my happiness. Their children are in the picture though. Occasionally the nieces and nephews did come to visit me. Now they will have to adjust to a new uncle. That is, they will have to adjust if their mothers will still let them come and visit me."

Judy's new marriage does affect her relationship with her family. A person's relationship with his or her family is constantly changing, however. No family can remain static. There is always change. Children start to school. Children become adolescents. Children marry. College, jobs, and military service affect families. Disease, disability, and ultimately death affect every family and every family member. Divorce and remarriage also fit into that pattern of constant change. Some relatives resist every change. They are determined to maintain certain family patterns and they are demoralized by inevitable change. Those relatives are the ones who will be most resistant to remarriage.

Other family members who can accept inevitable change may resist the divorce and remarriage for other reasons. They may have firm religious convictions about remarriage and divorce. Those religious convictions may be supported by family pride. The relatives may feel that divorce is a failure and they transfer the personal failure and adopt it as a family failure. There may be some family members like Judy's grandmother who endured an unhappy marriage and who think others should do the same.

Judy will have to accept some change in her personal relationship with her relatives. It will not be the same, but that is not necessarily bad. She may be able to enjoy a new kind of personal freedom and responsibility within her family that was impossible when the family controlled her life.

Ralph also faces some new relationships. He has a new set of in-laws who are not at all pleased with his introduction into the family. They may be courteous, or they may be cool. Either way, Ralph is thrust into an uncomfortable position. Even when the family "understands" the reasons for a divorce, they are often hesitant and reluctant to approve of the remarriage.

Ralph has a new family. He must accomodate their personal feelings and he has also been forced into the family traditions. Those family traditions may surface on holidays. Holidays will be one of the most difficult adjustments for Ralph and Judy.

Which family do you visit at Christmas? What about gifts? How can Ralph go to Indiana with Judy for her traditional Christmas celebration and see his children, who live with their mother in Virginia? Holidays and birthdays can strain the new marriage.

There are other family traditions and family expectations that Ralph and Judy will encounter during their marriage. Ralph has traditionally met his parents in the Smoky Mountains on vacations. Judy's family expects her to come home on her vacation. There are other special events that are common to the families. All of these things must be worked out in a spirit of compromise and good humor. Ralph and Judy must decide what traditions they can maintain and what traditions they can discard. It is not possible to keep everything like it was; some change and compromise is necessary. They should be able to work it out together, if they do not exaggerate the importance of the conflict.

Ralph and Judy and any couple involved in a new marriage face some difficult times when certain special events take place like weddings and funerals. Eventually Ralph's children will marry and the role of the absent

parent and the stepparents is always a special consideration in the wedding plans. Someone will have to decide
where Ralph and Judy fit in at that wedding.

As divorce has become more prevalent, the embarrass-
ment at these weddings has been diminished and arrangements are easier to handle. Nevertheless, it is one
of the dramatic reminders to everyone that the family
changed with the second marriage. At times there is no
easy way to work it out. One of the parents may be bitter
and angry and refuse to participate in the wedding if the
former mate is even invited. The problem may be in de-
ciding who gives the bride away, or who sits on which
side, or who stands where in the reception line, or who
sits on which pew in the church. New sets of stepgrand-
parents may further complicate the wedding.

Every pastor has been involved in these kinds of sticky
weddings where the entire atmosphere was marred by
battling adults and grieving children. But this happens
less often and the older adults seem more willing to
realize that the couple getting married should have a
peaceful ceremony that is not disrupted by quarreling,
hypersensitive parents.

A funeral can also produce some trauma. If the deceased did not approve of the new marriage, the death
can easily produce an unusual amount of guilt. If Judy's
grandmother were to die soon, unless Judy had made a
good attempt at reconciliation, Judy will have some
problems adjusting to her Grandma's death. Funerals
that involve the relatives of the former spouse also can
be uncomfortable. But the new marriage means change.
A funeral means a final change, and regardless of the relationship with the deceased or the other mourners, a
funeral is inevitable. As we mature, we learn that we
cannot build our relationships upon the inevitability of
death. There is more to life than the anticipation of funerals. Funerals will, however, be another event that
must be handled.

"They always say that you don't know someone until you live with them. Well, Ralph and I haven't lived together. He suggested a dozen times that we move in together. It's not a big point of contention. Ralph says that we could know one another better, and I guess he is right. We also could be together more and we could save money. But my conscience just won't let me do it. I'll admit that I have stayed all night with him more than once, and we have taken three or four week-end trips together. I rationalize about that, but I just can't live with him until we have the license. Sure, it's just a piece of paper, but it's a piece of paper that I must have before we live together.

"Anyway, the more time we spend together, the more sure I am that I love him. I want to live with him. I want to marry him and I want the marriage to work. But I'm scared. I don't think I felt that way when I married the first time, but I could have. Now, how can I be sure that Ralph and I won't aggravate one another?

"There is so much to adjust to. Our families, our friends, and most importantly one another. We have to adjust to eccentricities and tastes. He likes things that I don't like. Country music, for instance. He likes politics and politics bore me. He likes to read and I like T.V. Now I know about these things that are dissimilar. Are there bigger and more important differences?"

Judy and Ralph will have to adjust to personal tastes. Any two people who live together must allow some diversity. Love and compatibility cannot be confused with identical tastes. Any healthy relationship allows, even encourages, diversity. When two become one, the two do not give up their identity. There is a prevalent myth about marriage that proposes unreal and unnecessary similarity of tastes. Two people do not have to agree on everything to be happy. Neither party in a happy marriage has to give up or renounce certain things they personally enjoy.

We have made "togetherness" an unrealistic idol in

marriage. A man does not have to go with his wife to an antique show. The husband does not have to be interested in tennis to be a good husband. The wife does not have to be a precinct worker for the Democrats, nor does she have to go to baseball games to prove their togetherness. There are times when they both need to pursue their own interests with the casual approval of the mate. They will not, need not, share everything to make the marriage work.

This kind of apprehension is present when a person marries the first time, but it increases when he or she thinks about the next marriage. Divorce has accented those differences and they make one reluctant to marry someone else. Like Judy, many people who face a new marriage become frightened about personal adjustments and differences. Although none of those differences seems important, there is the lingering fear that any or all of them might become an insurmountable obstacle to happiness.

There must be things that you and your new mate agree on and enjoy together, or you would not even be discussing marriage. You are attracted to each other. You have things in common or you would not be this far along in discussing marriage. Keep your sense of balance. Do not ignore the differences, but do not exaggerate them. If your mutual interests are superior to your differences, you are all right.

However, there is the possibility that some differences are so profound and so important that they cannot be overlooked or hidden. If there is some area of conflict that simply cannot be overcome, then you should postpone indefinitely any plans for marriage to that person. Do not expect to reform or change him. Unless you can accept the differences without worry or the desire to reform him, don't marry him. Life is too short and happiness too elusive to spend time trying to reform a reluctant convert.

# "Have you met Ann?"

"I keep thinking about taking Ann places with me, and saying a dozen times, 'Have you met Ann?' " Dick is planning to marry Ann after a twenty-year marriage to Nancy that broke up in divorce about sixteen months ago. Dick is a busy, gregarious, well-liked man who has many friends in the city where he lives.

"I'm the kind of person who must be around other people. I like people. I need people. There is no way that I can live like a hermit. All of my life I've enjoyed a crowd more than I enjoy being alone, or even being alone with a woman I love. I would rather eat in a restaurant than in a private dining room. I would rather go to a football game with fifty thousand people than go out on a lonely pond fishing.

"A crowd of people excites me. So, I arrange my life to accomodate that excitement and stimulation. And I don't want to move that way alone. I want to take my wife along. I want her to meet my friends and be seen by people. She is an attractive woman and I want them to admire her like I do. There's no way that I can get away from people and no way that I want to.

"But I keep wondering about it. Nancy didn't enjoy it as much as I did, but she did go places with me. She liked some of the travel, some of the conventions, and some of the social life we had. She enjoyed it less as the years passed and eventually this became one of the points of contention between us. There were other, more serious ones, but this was certainly one of our problems. She thought that all of that extroverted behavior was shallow and was a cop-out on my part. It may be. But it is me. Be that as it is, Nancy went often enough and we were married long enough that people knew she was my wife. That was our identity, husband and wife, and I don't think she was ever ashamed of it.

"Now I'm thinking about taking Ann to those places and to those events. I'm self-conscious about introducing her to all of those people as my 'new' wife. It's awkward for her. And if I don't say she is my new wife, the people who know Nancy will think I'm running around with Ann, or they will think I'm ashamed of her."

Everyone who marries a second time has to go through the introducing stages. It begins with the family and the intimate friends and it continues for months and even years. The older someone is when he or she remarries and the larger the circle of friends and acquaintances, the more often the "let me introduce you to Ann" routine will have to be repeated.

This is necessary and it is not necessarily embarrassing. It only becomes embarrassing when one tries to ignore the social graces and/or tries to deceive. A new marriage is a legitimate relationship and it must be handled as such. There is no reason to withdraw from friends or other social opportunities. The introductions will probably not have to be repeated to the same people and most of them will accept or reject the new spouse on his or her personal attributes, not on the number of times either partner has been married. To coin a phrase, honesty is the best policy.

It may not work out that easily in the church or a business setting, or any other smaller group. Church people can be harsh about remarriage. This is unfortunate, but true. They may make a new partner uncomfortable and unwelcome. The church may be the most difficult place for remarried people to find acceptance, when it should be the easiest place.

The church has traditionally, and correctly, stood for marriage "till death do us part." No other institution has been as firm and as unyielding in that position as the church. Church influence has kept strict divorce laws on the books, and when divorce became easier by law, some churchmen became more rigid in practice.

Some churches have called divorce sin. Some have said it is unforgivable. Others have said divorce could be forgiven, but remarriage could not. Church dogma, church rules, and church attitudes have been enforced by twenty centuries of sermons denouncing divorce and remarriage, not as failure, but as sin.

Churches have adopted rules that support the "remarriage is sinful" position. They will not allow divorced and/or remarried people to be ordained to the clergy or ordained to certain lay positions. They deny the sacraments to divorced and/or remarried persons. They will not allow these people to hold church offices, or sing in the choir, or serve as ushers. Categories are often established that allow the divorced/remarried person to hold church membership but not church office.

Some clergymen have gone a step farther. They have not only supported these rules and regulations, but they have developed rather elaborate explanations that excuse them from performing weddings for people who are divorced. Some clergymen will perform the ceremony if "there is a scriptural reason for divorce." They mean if it can be "proven" that the divorced person was previously married to an adulterer. They never explain just how they determine the fact of adultery, but the reasoning apparently satisfies their own consciences.

All of this conspires together to make the church traditionally rigid about divorce and remarriage. With this kind of established position it is difficult for individual church members to treat a divorced or remarried person with warmth and love. Even when church members want to do this, they have some vague feeling that somehow it is just not right to treat divorced or remarried people as other human pilgrims. Consequently, they are uptight and self-conscious and often make remarried couples feel more uncomfortable. This is more than unfortunate; it directly violates the mission of the church.

Some church members react with suspicion because they think a divorced or remarried person has sinned. If they are honest, they know that they have sinned, too. But divorce and remarriage is a matter of public record. Most sins are not documented at the Courthouse. Their sins probably have not been made public record. No one but God will forgive theirs. God may forgive those who have divorced or remarried, but they won't. If they can escape public scrutiny with their private greed, private lust, private hatred and private self-righteousness, they will not allow the public fact of remarriage to go unpunished. So they treat the remarried person badly.

Others are not critical, but envious. Their envy is quickly transformed into hostility. All of us know people who are locked into a miserable marriage. A horribly unhappy marriage. But they do not break out of that misery. They stay married. When they see someone who did divorce and who has apparently found happiness in a new marriage, the envy spills over into a torrent of anger. Some of the people who treat a remarried person unkindly are envious of their apparent happiness.

Church people may be mean to a remarried couple, but that couple needs the church and the church needs that remarried couple. These two facts are more important than the immediate reaction of the people or the inflexible position of the church. A remarried couple must not give in to the pettiness and the non-Christian dogmatism that may seem prevalent. There is more at stake here than is immediately felt by the remarried couple or the dogmatic churchmen.

It is understandable when the remarried and the church seem to be entrenched behind fences, but it is not right for the persons involved. And it is inconsistent with the Christian faith and the redemptive ministry of the church. It is more than unfortunate; it is tragic. The remarried and the church must make serious and thoughtful attempts to reapproach the questions of divorce, remarriage and the Biblical idea of monogamy until death do us part.

The remarried person should take the initiative in the church by continuing his normal worship and service routines. This is not easy in a conservative church that frowns on remarriage. It may be embarassing. Any kind of judgment is unwelcome and this kind of religious judgment is especially distasteful. The remarried person who wants to continue his relationship with the church must patiently endure some of the "judgment". It won't last long, because people who are inclined to judge others always have new people to judge. Having "dealt with" the newly-remarried couple, they will move on to someone else who has erred by their standards. A remarried person needs just to be patient.

He or she cannot and need not explain the divorce and remarriage to friends or to church members. No explanation is necessary. A marriage that did not work is the obvious reason for a divorce. Trying to tell one side of the story will just complicate the attempt to function normally. The fact of the second marriage is a personal matter between the new marriage mates. Any attempts to explain what has happened just cheapens the intimate relationship between the new husband and wife. Explanations do not alleviate the temporary embarassments that the new marriage will produce.

Of course a person's life is changed by a new marriage. The change is for the better. The divorce is painful, but the divorce is over. The divorced person has chosen a new mate and is beginning a new life. There is no need to act arrogant, but neither is there need to be defensive. A remarried person should walk with a steady step, hold his or her head up, move into this new time of life with confidence. The happiness the new marriage promises must not be distorted by the behavior of others. There will be some bad moments in relating to other people, but these moments will pass if they are not allowed to get out of proportion. So much of the adjustment in this period depends upon attitude. If a remarried person acts confident, critics and the curious will soon forget the remarriage. The best is yet to be.

Mike had been reared in the church and had been chosen in his adult years to fill several important church assignments. He was by any standard an active layman. When Mike and Linda were divorced after ten years of marriage, the divorce came as a shock to most of the church members. Mike and Linda attended church regularly and they worked in the church. Most members equated that with a happy marriage. After the divorce Linda moved back to her native state of South Carolina and Mike kept coming to church and working in the church.

There were those people who speculated about the causes of the divorce. Some couples in the church who had been friends with Mike and Linda felt uncomfortable with Mike alone. There were some rumors that spread through the church about both Mike and Linda. It was a topic of concern and conversation in the church, but Mike largely ignored the conversation and went on in the church in his normal way. Some of the people said that Mike "acted like nothing had happened." This was not true. Something had happened, but Mike felt confident about his decision to divorce and he was determined to maintain some dignity and to maintain his role in his church.

After several months, the people accepted Mike as he was and they saw him basically as they had always seen him. He was a faithful church member who willingly accepted the particular responsibilities that he was able to carry out.

When Mike began bringing a young woman to church the people were curious again. He introduced her to the people comfortably and most of them accepted her as a person. There were some difficult experiences, of course, but most of the people graciously accepted Mike's new friend. The people began to assume that Mike would marry her, and when the wedding was announced, the church responded gladly. Mike and his new wife were graciously accepted and they continue to work in the church and receive the blessings of worship without embarassment.

Mike is fortunate in several ways. He had been reared in that church and his former wife had moved away. They did not have to decide which one would attend which church. He also could rely on people who had known him for most of the years of his life. His new wife also helped because she believed that the church was important and was willing to go along with him and patiently win the affection and respect of the church members.

But more than any of these factors, Mike handled the crisis of the divorce and remarriage in the right way. He did not "tell his story." He did not try to explain his divorce or remarriage. He did not seek pity nor revenge. He conducted himself with dignity and self-confidence and this impressed people. Mike wanted to stay in church. He wanted to worship God in his church and he wanted to work in the church as he always had. He wanted this enough to stick with it when it would have been easier to quit. He believed in it enough to overcome his critics and the gossips by quietly showing up for worship and by effectively doing the things he was asked to do.

It is easy for divorced and remarried people to give up on the church, and give up on friends. There is some embarassment involved. People can be critical, even harsh. It is easier to drop all of the relationships of the past, including the church, than it is to face them and patiently rebuild some torn bridges. We always lose some self-respect when we give up. We always lose something when we give in to unfair criticism. We always lose when we drop out of the important institutions and important relationships. It may be tough to maintain some of these important relationships from the past, but the maintenance is worth the cost. A remarried person can keep his or her self-respect by not yielding to group pressure, even when it is done in the name of religion.

# "I keep comparing Mike and Lewis"

When a person gets married for the first time he or she tends to compare the marriage to his or her parents' marriage. When that person marries a second time, he or she is inclined to compare the new marriage to the previous one. If the new mate has been married before, the same thing is going on with him or her. This is to be expected. It is a normal reaction to new experiences. We compare.

No two people are exactly alike. It is often said that men marry women who are like their mothers and that women marry men who are like their fathers. Sometimes they do, and sometimes they marry people who are not at all like their parents. Some people who marry again choose people who are similar to the person they divorced. Some choose a person who is obviously different from their previous mate. Even when those kinds of decisions are thought out and premeditated, no two people are exactly alike, and the new marriage involves a new partner in a new situation.

This all means that there will be comparisons. The comparisons cannot be avoided, but they can be handled in a mature way. They can strengthen and support the new marriage or they can be a source of conflict and frustration, especially in sexual relationships.

"When I was a teenager growing up in church groups and church camps, I was told that sex was something special for a man and woman who really were in love and who were married," Lee begins. Lee is in his thirties, an attorney with a successful law firm. He has been married about two years to his second wife. His first marriage lasted about twelve years.

"We were taught that all kinds of heavy petting were wrong because that would get you too excited and you might have premarital sex. Premarital sex was bad. It was wrong. It was sinful. In fact, in my church and my circle of teenage friends, there was an intense preoccupation with sex. I'm not sure how many of the kids actually had sex, but it was on everyone's mind. When we had church meetings they talked to us all of the time about staying pure, don't get into trouble, don't 'go too far' and all of that kind of thing. If the teenagers didn't have sex on their minds, the youth counselors did.

"We equated premarital sex with sin. If one of our group was uptight about something in a church meeting, the assumption was that he or she had been involved in some sex escapade. We were also taught that God would punish premarital sex. Of course they warned us about unwanted pregnancies, about venereal diseases, and other ominous possibilities. But the main threat was that God would get you.

"You were not to experiment with sex because God would zap you. I had the feeling as a teenager that God did nothing but watch with his all-seeing eye to find out who was sneaking around to have sex. And when he caught you in some illicit sex act, he would get you.

"My youth counselors used another approach, too. They not only tried to frighten us about premarital sex, but they also told us that we would never enjoy sex unless we had it with the 'right' person. The 'right' person of course was the one that we were married to. They always talked about the 'right' person and the 'right' time. This always meant sex in marriage.

"Like most young people, I soon found out that my counselors were not telling me all of the truth. Eventually young people in high school, college, military service, or somewhere, usually experiment and get involved in some love affairs. They find out that God doesn't zap them out with heart attacks or V.D. or paralysis. They wait for him to do them in and it doesn't happen.

"And they find out that sex can be enjoyable and have meaning even when you do not get married. Even when you do not plan to get married. Sex can be desirable outside of marriage."

Lee continued, "Not that I've had sex with a lot of different women. My point is that sex is a terribly strong and natural desire. That desire can not be restricted by religious rules, especially when they are simply not true. People in the church lie a lot about sex and young people know, or soon learn, what is true and what is false. If we are going to have any sex education in the church, it must be honest.

"Anyway, I found out that sex is not reserved for marriage. Not only is premarital sex a fact of life, but extramarital sex is also a fact of life. Everyone knows that. People know something else about sex. A lot of men and women get involved in sex affairs and they don't plan to get involved. We talk a lot about people being 'on the make,' and some are. They are always looking for a new person to go to bed with. There are others who end up in bed and they didn't plan it that way, they weren't on the make at all. It just happened because sex is so strong.

"I'm not trying to make an apology for free love or for extramarital affairs. My concern is that we set sex in a proper perspective. I know that people can have sex without fear, sex without guilt, sex without marriage and sex without love.

"What does that do to sex in marriage? Sex and love? I did not ever love my first wife like I love my present wife. When I married the first time I was making a marriage that everyone thought was proper; it was an expected and approved marriage. My first wife, Mary, was from the same kind of family I was from. We had been reared in the same kind of community, same kind of church, same kind of economic situation. We were very much alike. We got along very well for four or five years. Our marriage in the early days was no better, no worse than others. When our marriage did begin to come apart, it was a slow but steady kind of unraveling. Finally there was nothing left.

"Now the sex thing comes in. Mary and I always had sex. We had sex after we had filed for divorce. I'm a lawyer and I handle divorce cases and I know that this was not exceptional with Mary and me. Other people who find they can't, or don't want to, live together can and do have sex together.

"About a year after my divorce I met Julie. We fell in love. I'm not sure what I mean by that, but we really love one another. We want to be together. We trust one another. We have fun together. It is just a great feeling. Nothing like this has ever happened to me before. We married about two years ago.

"Sex with Julie is a different kind of thing. I have a different feeling for Julie than I had for Mary. It is not the question of sex technique, frequency of sex—those kinds of things. It is all wrapped up in my feelings. My feelings for Julie are at the same time more intense and more tender, more passionate and more reserved. I am happy with Julie. Really happy! But I do compare my sex life with Julie to my sex life with Mary. Julie is not Mary. Mary is not Julie. Sex is different with Julie because I love her."

Lee is uncomfortable with his comparisons. Sex is always intimate and personal. Sex is never the same. There is a kind of biological behavior in sex that has sameness to it, but sex is never just a biological act. There is always attitude and feeling involved. This is the most important part of sex; it expresses the way a person feels toward someone he or she loves.

It has been said that some people can have sex anytime, anyplace. But that isn't true. There are certain physical limitations that make sex impossible. Extreme fatigue, or pain, or other temporary physical liabilities will prohibit sex. Psychological factors also limit sexual activity. Anxiety, fear, disgust, or preoccupation will make one impotent or disinterested. We all know that sexual activities will be limited at times.

Comparisons do affect sex. No two people respond to sex in identical ways. They do not express their sexual needs in the same way. They are physically and emotionally responsive to different kinds of sex play. They have different needs at different times. They do different things with their body, they make different sounds, they find different satisfactions. These differences force the comparisons.

After twelve years of marriage to Mary, Lee knew something about her responses. There was a kind of familiarity and understanding in their sex life. His initial experiences with Julie were exciting partly because they were different. It was a change. The change itself added to the attraction.

Lee has had some variety of sexual experience in his life. With the exception of Mary and Julie, it has always been casual. There was no commitment. He did not really care. He had not given much thought to what was going on in the sex act. He was not trying to impress the woman involved and he was not willing to be impressed. These casual affairs were not frequent, but they had happened often enough for him to be accustomed to the "variety" experience.

Extramarital sex is not fulfilling because it is not a natural way to express love. The sexual activist may be on an ego trip; he may be accumulating conquests like the frontier gunman notched his gun. He may be just searching for a "new" feeling. The promiscuous person is at best pitiful and is always doing the wrong things the wrong way.

But even many adults who never have an "affair" are attracted to the "variety" idea. They think about, fantasize, an affair with someone else. They speculate, wonder what it would be like to go to bed with someone else. Some people in counseling admit that when they have sex with their husband or wife, they fantasize that it is someone else. It is usually someone they know and they are attracted to.

Again all of this variety, in fact or fantasy, only points up the complex attitudes and feelings most people have about sex and the importance of love in marriage. These complex feelings are accented in that new marriage. The second marriage is a legal and legitimate relationship. It is not a casual affair. It is not a clandestine meeting in a hotel. It is not a secret dream or an erotic fantasy. It is an established relationship. Marriage channels the sex drive.

Comparing the sexual responses in a second marriage with the former marriage is inevitable. The problem Lee has is typical in a new marriage. He will have to learn about Julie, just like he had to learn about Mary when they first married. Sex is always more than doing "what comes naturally." Any loving, sensitive person tries to make sex mutually satisfying. There is some art in being a good lover. Because someone else is always involved, and involved at a deep emotional level, the successful lover is never casual. He never comes to sex casually or carelessly.

I believe that the comparisons can be helpful if kept in perspective. The comparisons should not be overemphasized. I doubt if any person is unresponsive to love, tenderness, and consideration. There are doubtlessly some people who are more sexually active than others. Some who are less modest, some who can respond more easily, some who can speak sex more easily. If a former marriage was more comfortable, the artful lover will try to privately determine what made it more comfortable.

Making comparisons to a new mate should be done very carefully, if ever. This is a most delicate area. I don't know very many people, regardless of their sophistication and smugness, who enjoy being compared to someone else in sex and marriage. There is always insecurity in a new marriage. Talking about a former mate, especially bedroom talk, adds to the insecurity.

If Mary did things in bed that enhanced Lee's sexual pleasure, he should gently and indirectly lead Julie that way. I think it is risky for Lee to tell Julie that Mary did certain things that he wants Julie to do. Lee and Julie can learn from each other and they can learn together. It is best for him to leave Mary out of his new marriage, especially out of his bed.

There are other kinds of comparisons that show up in a second marriage. The remarried couple will have to decide how much of this they will talk about and how much they will ignore.

"I'm happier now than I was," Barbara began, "but I keep comparing Mike and Lewis. Lewis and I were married for four years. The four years seemed like twenty. Lewis was a drag. He is a late edition of the gray flannel suit man. Lewis went to work twenty minutes before the office opened. He worked after the other office staff left for home. He felt guilty taking off work for holidays or vacation. He is the complete and ideal organization man. If they told him to do it, he did it. No one in his office would question his loyalty, his dedication, or his dependability. At the same time, no one would expect him to have a new idea or to engage in office politics.

"Lewis was domesticated. He liked to eat at home, although we would occasionally go out. If we had friends in, or went to visit anyone, Lewis would plan the social event in detail. He would plan a dinner like it was D-Day. Every detail and every possibility had to be considered days in advance.

"He enjoyed the house and yard. He had a five-year plan for landscaping. The painting, maintenance, and repair was always done and done on schedule. We replaced furniture and light bulbs on schedule. He helped me around the house willingly. Dishes. Cleaning. The house was his castle, and the castle was cared for.

"As you can imagine, his behavior was also carefully controlled. We never had a fight. We never even had an argument. He would walk out when I would throw a fit.

He didn't laugh much. I never saw him cry. He didn't raise his voice in excitement or anger. His hands didn't shake. I don't think anyone would ever say that Lewis was upset about anything.

"Lewis did not believe in controversy or confrontation. He sincerely believed that everyone had a good side and that they had good qualities. He believed there were two sides to every argument and every controversy. He held no strong opinions and expressed none. Lewis had so much self-control that he became a bore, a blasé person who nearly drove me crazy.

"So I married Mike. Mother said I was trading a sunset for an atomic blast. That's about it. Mike is self-employed. He struggles with his schedule. He is very successful in his work, but his schedule is hectic. I can't count on him to be home at any set time. He sleeps late, stays up late. Then he changes and gets up before dawn and comes home in mid-afternoon.

"Mike has an opinion about anything. He is a compulsive talker and an interesting conversationalist. He can be loud, witty, or confidential. He raves and rants. People make him angry. I make him angry. His feelings are always open. He apologizes quickly. He weeps. He loves me and tells me so. He is excitable and enthusiastic, or moody and withdrawn. People feel strongly about Mike. I'm never quite sure just what his current relationship is with certain people.

"He has a casual interest in our house and yard. He isn't domesticated at all and at times I think he would never notice dirty dishes, a leaking roof, or a tree on the front porch. He gives me money and never questions my use of it. He doesn't really care about money. Lewis kept our finances like he was expecting the FBI to check his records.

"I'm happy with Mike. But at times I feel like I'm on a roller coaster. Lewis bored me and Mike keeps me constantly off base."

Barbara has been married to extremes and she will always make comparisons. Comparisons are inevitable. Most people who remarry do not choose the extremes that Lewis and Mike represent. Many people, in fact, marry someone who is similar to their former mate. Those comparisons are subtle. Other divorcees do marry opposites. Like Barbara they are attracted to people who are dramatically different from their former mates. These comparisons between opposites are not subtle, but they can strain the new marriage.

I have known people who think that the best way to compliment anyone is by making comparisons. "You are better looking than your father." "You play golf better than your big brother." "You sing better than your Aunt Lucy." "You learned to talk before your sister." A lot of this goes on in a family. It usually breeds an unhealthy sense of competition and always puts someone down in the process of building up someone else.

There is an attraction to competition and winners and losers are part of the national scene. We expect it in athletics, beauty contests, and political races. Competition is necessary in a free enterprise system and is expected in a tennis tournament. But it is not helpful or constructive in a marriage. Spoken and discussed comparisons invariably put the new marriage into the realm of competition and contest where the new marriage partner must compete as a replacement for the "ex." It is extremely unfair because the "ex" is not present for the contest. There is just the imperfect memory of the husband or wife who is trying to make these comparisons.

The new wife does not respond sexually the same way the "ex" responded. There will also be differences in spending habits, housekeeping habits, taste in clothes and food, laughter, and religion. There will be differences in the way the grass is cut, the kinds of friends, and the way vacations are spent. There are differences to be expected and enjoyed.

All comparisons, subtle or obvious, are not bad. There were problems in the former marriage or there would

93

not have been a divorce. The new mate will compare favorably in most areas. The new mate will excel in others. One of the reasons for divorce and remarriage is to make improvements in the marriage relationship.

A man who was married to a caustic woman hopefully will not marry another caustic woman. A woman formerly married to an ambitious, self-centered man will not make the same mistake. A religious woman formerly married to an agnostic will not marry another irreligious man. A sexually active man who has been married to a passive woman hopefully will not do it again.

Comparisons can be a trap. They are inevitable, but they must be kept in perspective. If the next marriage succeeds, comparisons should be made positively. The new partner has many good qualities compared to the former partner. But they should not be discussed unless a severe crisis develops and must be talked out. It is important to be cautious with comparisons.

# IV.
# It Can Work!

# "I've learned my lesson!"

One of the primary reasons that remarriage works is because people who have been previously married learn and mature from the prior marriage experience. Everyone at any given time is the sum total of his experience. Even if the prior marriage was a failure in most areas, it was, or should have been, a learning experience. And that experience adds to the potential for happiness in the new marriage.

"When I married the first time, I married for the wrong reasons. I had never been very happy at home with my parents. They got along with each other well enough and they treated me OK. They both worked and worked hard. We didn't do much as a family and didn't talk much. I don't think either of my parents thought that I was unhappy. They would be surprised now if they knew that I had wanted to get away from home.

"Boys in my generation left home easier than girls did. Boys went away to work, or they went into military service, or they went to college. They got away. I did not want to go to college and there were plenty of jobs in my hometown. It looked to me like marriage was the best way to leave home and get out on my own.

"I didn't know much about marriage. But I knew that I wanted to leave home, so I married." Linda is in her mid-twenties and has been divorced for about eighteen months. The marriage she has just described lasted about six years. It was never a strong or happy marriage. It was never a bitter or hostile marriage. Linda and her husband had no strong feelings about each other and no strong commitment to marriage. It wasn't casual, but it wasn't very important to either of them.

People have always married for the wrong reasons. This starts the marriage off with a severe disability. Occasionally the couple can overcome that disability, but most often it does permanent, if not terminal, damage to the marriage. Getting married for the wrong reasons is one of the primary causes for divorce. It helps when contemplating remarriage to look at the reasons for a new marriage.

Linda wanted to leave her parents and get out on her own; she was not happy with her parents. That is often the case. Marriage is an excuse to cut the apron strings. Most parents think that their children will marry and they are prepared to some degree for that to happen. Consequently marriage is one of the best and most acceptable ways to leave the parental nest with a minimum of hassle from Mom and Dad.

Linda also wanted some freedom and she felt that she had to leave home to get it. Other young people seeking the privilege of adult life leave home and go on their own in other ways. But marriage is still the most popular, and again the most acceptable, way to get that kind of adult freedom. If "being free" is the reason for marriage, the young bride and groom soon find that they may be free of parental and/or hometown restrictions, but marriage has its own confining boundaries and freedom becomes a relative thing.

When Linda marries again these two ideas will be behind her. She has already left home and that trauma is over. Her parents and Linda have already established a new relationship. This is entirely different than it was when she married the first time. Linda has also had a taste of "adult freedom" and the corresponding responsibility. The new marriage does not have the intriguing possibility of "freedom" that she expected the first time.

Linda married for wrong reasons the first time, but she has learned. It is to be hoped that she will marry for the right reasons the next time. At least she is not trying to escape her parents or to find freedom. She is no longer a child. She is not going out on her own for the first time. That is a big advantage over her first marriage.

"Although Alice and I had gone through college together before we married, and although we had a rather lengthy courtship of more than eighteen months, we never really had the same set of values. I had always wanted to be successful. I thought she did. I enjoyed money and prestige. I thought she did. And she did. She liked our big house, our big cars, our long trips, the things money bought her.

"It takes hard work to get that kind of money and my kind of reputation. I didn't inherit money, so I worked harder than most men to get it. And I got it! We had plenty. We were wealthy by most standards in our city. People respected us and we moved with the classy crowd. Sure, it costs time. The time when I could have been at home I spent earning money.

"Eventually Alice wanted the time and the money. She couldn't have it both ways. I simply could not give her time and still earn the money we spent. That produced all kinds of conflict. She started accusing me of buying her and trying to keep her bought. She asked me to change jobs, live on less, give up my ambition for her and the kids. I kept saying she didn't really mean it. Finally I knew she did mean it and found out to my dismay that I was locked in. I wasn't doing it for her. I was doing it for me and I wasn't willing to change. Didn't want to change. So we divorced. And I still work too many hours, too many days and spend too much money.

"Alice and I did not have any agreement about this kind of thing. I guess we both assumed that there would never be any conflict between my career and our marriage. We both assumed that we wanted the same thing as far as money and prestige was concerned. We found out too late that this wasn't true. I don't think it was ever true. I don't think we ever shared the same sense of values about the importance of money and social standing. I really believe that Alice would have been satisfied, even happy, in a three-room apartment married to a common laboring man if he would have stayed at home with her. She wanted a man who would take her bowling, a man who would plant some trees and cut the grass, a man who would wander in a discount store for three hours, a man who would like to go on picnics. She needed a man around who could be perfectly satisfied with a regular check, membership in the Lions Club, a glass of beer, and a pet dog.

"There is no way that I fit that mold. I don't have it in me. I didn't want it and don't want it now. It sounds horrible and wasteful to me."

Alice and her former husband made a mistake when they married. He assumed that every woman wanted to be married to a successful achiever. He assumed that every woman wanted trips to Europe, big houses, big bank accounts, and social standing. Many women also assume that, but they do not count the cost. That kind of life normally extracts dues. Those who attain that standard of living pay for it in an enormous expenditure of personal time. A family gives up certain "typical" family things for that kind of achievement.

If Alice's husband falsely assumed she wanted that kind of expensive life, Alice apparently falsely assumed that she could live in elegance without giving up some of her husband's time and concentration. They never seriously talked about this profound conflict of values until it was too late.

When Alice and her former husband plan to marry again they will not make that same mistake. They will both face these facts with the person they want to marry. They will talk about money, about work schedule, about social standing. They will focus upon this important kind of life value and they will reconcile it prior to marriage. They will avoid making false assumptions about important things.

We can expect people who married for the wrong reasons and people who assumed the wrong things to correct these errors the second time they marry. We expect them to have learned something from the first marriage. They will also have learned something about marriage. A marriage and a divorce usually bring the whole idea of marriage into the realm of realism. A prior marriage and divorce force a person to look at the institution of marriage clearly. Romantic idealism and dreamy fantasy are brought into the real world. The person who marries again is not apt to be idealistic or naive.

This realism is necessary in a working marriage. Marriage is always a tough relationship. Unfortunately, most people are poorly prepared for the tough part. When things get hard, they want to get out. If they have married and are essentially convinced that marriage is a continuous honeymoon, they are hurt when they find the honeymoon is over. If they have expected every conflict to end in a fond embrace and a Hollywood reconcilation, they are shocked at the reality of conflict. Some people never forget the first fight. They did not expect it and were absolutely incompetent to handle it. The person who marries again understands that there are some tough times ahead in any marriage and is ready to handle them. Even if he can't handle them well, he is at least not surprised when they happen.

"I don't think I understood, until it was too late, just how involved your life is with your wife." Ted is a former minister who is divorced and planning a new marriage. "I was reared with a certain amount of independence. I was encouraged by my parents to develop my own personal interests, my own talents, and my own goals. I wasn't really a loner, but I did like privacy. I am not a fanatic, but I am strongly opinionated. I like to have my own way, but never insist that everyone do things my way or go along with me. In fact I prefer that people, instead of tagging along, just stay out of my way. I'm not very good with people who interfere, interrupt or intervene. That is, I know, a kind of selfish and self-centered behavior. It did not work in the church. I developed a lot of resentment toward the church people who kept interrupting my life. It was eventually a catastrophe in our marriage. My wife kept telling me that we were involved in all of it together. She was right. A husband is not the Lone Ranger with some mumbling, acquiescent Tonto trailing him at a discreet, nonverbal distance.

"This whole question of our mutual involvement and mutual dependence was the thing that finally destroyed our marriage. Now as I plan another marriage, I am more aware of our mutual involvement. I've learned my lesson!"

Ted probably has learned his lesson. And the lesson must be learned. No man is an island. That means no husband and no wife is an island. The clear implication of the Bible idea of "the two become one" is tied up in this involvement. Some couples who are comfortable and very loving can respect, even encourage a lot of individuality. There is less talk today about togetherness and that is good. It has never been necessary for husband and wife to share every minute or agree on every question and opinion.

Keeping our individuality and honoring our involvement is a delicate balancing act. There are no formulas. There is no neat way to arrange it. It is essential in a working marriage to recognize involvement. What your mate does, what he thinks, the way he uses his time, the way he spends money, what he believes, and what you do with one another does affect both of you. Even when both parties agree to go their separate ways and stay married while doing it, they are both involved in that kind of marriage behavior. Ted learned in his first marriage that he could not ignore the emotional and physical involvement that marriage produces.

Sue is an active church member. She has always been involved in the music program in the church and is a popular singer. She is talented and her music has been her primary achievement. Sue is not particularly attractive, but she has good presence when she sings. Her music has affected her image and it has affected her self-esteem. She had sung at church, school, and in community programs since her early teens, and this had been her role. She had never considered singing professionally and had always planned to marry and have children.

When Sue and Joe married, everyone in the church thought it was an ideal marriage. Six years and two children later, Sue and Joe divorced, and now Sue is planning to marry again.

"I learned more about myself in six years of marriage than I would have believed possible. Sure, I learned a lot about Joe. About having babies and rearing children. And I think I know now what marriage is. But most of all, I learned about myself.

"Being married to Joe taught me that I am not on stage all of the time. With me it was singing, but I think most people try to be on stage. They want to act life out. They want applause and approval. Everyone wants to be in the spotlight. When I was married I realized that I wanted that spotlight and wasn't really willing to share it with Joe or my own children. I needed to learn that. Marriage taught me that about myself.

"I learned that life is more than being in the spotlight. It is more than recognition and compliments. All of us want recognition. I had always received it because of my music. Joe also wanted some compliments. I found out that there were certain duties in a marriage that you had to do without compliments or recognition or even thanks.

"This experience in my first marriage taught me that a mature person does what she has to do whether she receives compliments and appreciation or not. I had to know that and I learned it.

"I also learned to be honest about my feelings. I had always wanted to be popular and be approved. When I was little, I found out the things that made my parents and other people happy with me. All through school I tried to get the approval of the other kids and the teachers. And it worked. I was always "Miss Popularity." Everyone thought that I was the easiest person in the world to get along with. I was always friendly, always smiling, always on stage.

"If I thought someone didn't like me, it would worry me to death. If someone disagreed with something I said, I would apologize and agree with them. I didn't have any strong feelings about anything because I was afraid that someone would disagree with me. Nothing was more important to me than what others thought of me.

"So if I was discouraged or disappointed, I wouldn't ever tell anyone. Wouldn't even admit it to myself. I wouldn't try to work through a perplexing problem; I would just leave the problem and hope it would go away. I would not allow myself to get angry. I never blew my cool, never lost my temper. Mother used to say that she had never seen me mad. I never admitted or talked about fear, frustration, anger, doubt, or love. My feelings frightened me and I ignored them. Well, marriage changed all of that. When I was married I quit pretending. Quit hiding my feelings. I tried to be honest with myself and with the kids. By that time, we were ready for a divorce. But in my next marriage I won't try to hide my feelings."

The next marriage has a better chance of success because the first marriage is teacher. Some people mature enough to learn from the past, especially from mistakes and failures of the past. It is to be hoped that learning about marriage and about oneself will be helpful and profitable in the new marriage.

# "The church can help"

Can a new marriage work? Yes, the new marriage can work, and the church can help. Although the church has traditionally been an institutional bulwark against divorce and remarriage, the church at the same time has the potential to aid and support the couple who do marry again. More and more the church is pointing her ministry toward newlywed people who have been married before.

Some churches, of course, still maintain a very rigid position in opposition to divorce and remarriage. These inflexible churches will not help the newlyweds early in their new marriage and will probably offer little help as the years pass. This very conservative position is based upon a simple equation: Divorce is wrong. Remarriage is wrong. The church cannot accept a person in that position. And the church is incapable of ministering to the person that the church cannot, or will not, accept.

While there are still too many churches in that category, there are many other churches that are person-centered and are able and willing to share their ministry with people who have been through a divorce and are trying to make a new start in a new marriage. Dramatic changes within the church are being made daily, changes that enlarge the scope and the impact of the church in our society.

The church can help guarantee the success of a second marriage by encouraging the couple to be married in the church building by the clergy. I can remember ten years ago when the location of a wedding was a big issue in certain churches. Some churches had rules that prohibited church weddings for people who were divorced. That question is rarely discussed now. If the church allows, even encourages, weddings in the sanctuary for people who have been married before, the church is helping the couple get started with a religious ceremony. Use of the building gives tacit approval, an implied blessing to the new marriage. Often a person who wants to be remarried will tell me that they were not married in a church the first time and they want the symbolism of a church wedding the next time.

The church can help when the pastor agrees to perform the wedding ceremony. People call me and, with some hesitancy and embarassment, ask me whether I will marry someone who has been married before. If I reject their invitation to minister in this way, simply because they have been married before, I have established a false and shallow critique of my office and my use of time. This is an abrupt and effective way to turn them away. Some ministers say "No, I never marry anyone who has been married before under any circumstances." I have a minister friend whose daughter was deserted by her husband. She wanted to marry again and her father, who approved enthusiastically of her prospective husband, still refused to perform the ceremony. It was a serious and lasting rejection by him which the daughter still resents.

This is not to suggest that a pastor should casually agree to perform weddings for anyone who asks. I have never had a wedding until and unless I have had an opportunity to talk with the couple. This "talk" may consist of several premarital counseling sessions; it may be involved, or it may be some review conversation. There is always a conference and that conference adds some dignity and meaning to the wedding ceremony. If the couple refuse to talk to me, then I refuse to conduct the wedding. This is not harsh, and it is necessary. My role in the wedding is more than reader of the ceremony; it is more than agent of the state, or representative of the church. The role is ministry, and ministry at least means that we know one another and that we have some agreement about the wedding itself and about the meaning of marriage.

The role of the minister with this couple may begin at a premarital conference, but hopefully that role will continue after the wedding. Some of the people who are remarried by the minister will be members of his church. In that case he is doing his pastoral assignment for church members. He has that kind of expected obligation. Others who come to him for remarriage are not members of his church. It is not uncommon for some of those people to join his church. All clergymen have had people whom he has married join his church at a later time.

Of course, a wedding is not a tool for recruiting church members. The worthy minister is always willing to minister to people who are not his church members. When he performs a wedding ceremony, he is putting himself in a position to help them as counselor, friend, and pastor the rest of their married life. I always tell them that my interest in their new home and new relationship does not end when I sign the license. My interest and desire to minister goes on after the wedding. If I am to be honored by participating in their life at the wedding, I certainly will be available in the months and years ahead.

Most modern clergymen have some training and a lot of experience in marriage and family counseling. Some churches have full-time trained counselors on their pastoral staff. This kind of ministry is important to the newlyweds. The family life minister on our church staff is an able young man who spends nearly all of his working hours giving guidance and help to married people. When people remarry and run into conflict, disappointment, and frustration, they can find family counseling services offered in many contemporary churches. This kind of ministry offers professional help at the time that it is needed. In this way the church can help make the new marriage work.

The church can minister to families and has usually been considered a partner to the family. New emphasis in the contemporary church on helping the family has been productive. There are family life workshops that deal with communication, conflict, and other important family concerns. Churches have small group programs that help husbands and wives clarify their marriage expectations and roles. In addition to small groups and workshops for husbands and wives, churches sponsor specialized kinds of family workshops. There are workshops for parents of elementary or preschool-age children, workshops for parents and teenagers. There is a new awareness in the church about her ministry to families and this awareness is expressed in these multiple programs, retreats, groups, and workshops. This kind of emphasis can help the people who remarry.

Our church began a program in 1967 for single parents. This program was designed for people who because of divorce, death, or separation were rearing children without a marriage partner. In a city of two hundred thousand, we have about three hundred people enrolled in some of the activities of that group. This response has been surprising! Most of these members have been divorced, and they are eager for this kind of group.

Although there are many secular groups for those single parents, a church group has some advantages over the secular groups. The major advantage is that the church, by sponsoring the group, is recognizing that those divorced people are in fact persons with worth and with need. They are not put off or put out by the church. They are accepted and they respond favorably to that.

Many of the people who are members of that single parent group decide to remarry. It would be inconsistent, if not absurd, for the church to minister to them during and after the divorce and then cut them off as persons when they remarry.

The church can help the couple who marries again by giving positive encouragement to them in their new marriage experience. This encouragement may come in specific ways such as personal counseling sessions or family workshops, but the church can also contribute in a broader, less specific way by modifying her attitude about remarriage and by being more temperate in her language.

The church has and should exert strong influence to maintain "till death do us part" as the norm for marriage. The biblical and ethical ideal is one man, one woman until death. The church has always been committed to that principal and has worked hard to strengthen that ideal. But the church can work for that kind of marriage and at the same time be less rigid about the remarriage of divorced persons. These two concepts are not mutually exclusive.

Certain church leaders are apparently incapable of adjusting the idealism of "till death parts us" to the fact of divorce and remarriage. This is unfortunate because it locks the church into a position that severely limits her ministry. This position automatically excludes thousands from the caring ministry of the church.

The church can change her attitude about the potential of a remarried person. It is almost always true that a clergyman who divorces and marries again is out of the ministry. In my church there are four men who have had reasonably successful ministerial assignments in the past, but were forced out of the ministry after a divorce and new marriage. Three of those four went back to school, after at least three years of postgraduate seminary training, and were graduated into another profession. All three of them say that they wish they had been able to continue in the pastoral ministry. I am impressed that three of those four men have unusual gifts for the ministry and the church is the loser because they were forced out.

The pastor of my home church when I was a boy was

divorced and remarried. He baptized me and ordained me. He was my model for the ministry, the only pastor I ever had because I left my home church to be a pastor. He was a pastor for more than sixty years and his record of leadership was distinguished by any standard. I have never been sure just how he survived with his divorce and remarriage, but I am profoundly grateful that some churches and some denominational leaders did not force him out of the ministry.

Churches have tolerated some mediocrity in the ministry. We have endured pastors who were lazy, inarticulate, incompetent, and who displayed no gifts for leadership. We have allowed shallow, inane preaching; we have allowed pastors to become ecclesiastical errand boys. We have eventually come to expect very little from our clergy. And we have gotten as little as we expected. But we have insisted that he be married to only one woman, and we have been terribly intolerant of divorce and remarriage. This attitude must change, and we must be willing to let remarried men use their pastoral gifts in the church.

This problem has not been confined to our clergy. We have also made remarried church members a part of the second team. Many churches will not elect divorced and remarried church members to their boards. These people cannot be deacons or elders. They cannot teach Sunday School classes, or usher, or sing in the choir. There is an enormous waste of talent and gifts in this kind of arbitrary classification. The church can not have different classifications of church members if the church is to function effectively in our society. The church must change her attitude, and often her rules, if she is to minister effectively to all people. All people includes the divorced and remarried.

In order to help new marriages work, the church must modify language. We can not encourage or help the remarried person if we equate divorce and remarriage with sin.

"I don't know what to do. My pastor says remarriage is a sin. So I'm living in sin. I've been married to Shirley for three years. We have a baby. My former wife is happily married and she has a baby by her new husband. So, do I quit living in sin by divorcing Shirley, leaving my baby, and trying to get my first wife to divorce her present husband and move back with me?

"Now if I keep on living with Shirley, and loving her, am I always living in sin? Is it sin all of the time or just sin when I have sex with her? Do I sin less by getting another divorce? And where is the teaching about forgiveness? Am I to assume that my remarriage, if it is sin, is the only sin in my life that can't be forgiven. The church acts like it is unforgivable because they always talk about the sin of divorce and remarriage. It confuses me and it irritates me. Who wants to be condemned as a perpetual sinner who has no chance for forgiveness?"

If the church is to help the remarried person, the church must be more temperate in her language. We can become glib and thoughtless in our language, especially our "sin" language. This kind of harsh language not only betrays human insensitivity but biblical ignorance. There is absolutely no biblical or theological evidence to suggest that any "sin" is unforgivable, unless the person refuses to ask for forgiveness. In the case where the rebellious person refuses to ask, all sin is unforgiven and no one thing is more serious than all of the rest. Jesus said that to break one part of the law was to break it all, and to ask forgiveness was to receive forgiveness. The Bible consistently rejects our human attempts to categorize "good sins" and "bad sins," "big sins" and "little sins," "long-term sins" and "short-term sins."

The church can help remarried persons because it offers them the kind of "family" that people need in our transient, changing society. One of the functions of the modern church is fellowship. Since World War II our population has shifted to the city. People have left the "home place" and they are living in metropolitan areas away from the old house, the grandparents, the familiar village, and the small church. This geographical change has had a tremendous effect upon the family and upon individuals.

Many of these uprooted people have found a new family and a new community in the church. The church organizations and meetings provide the "causes" they need. The church people are the social contacts they need. They visit church members who are ill, they go to funeral homes when church members have had a death, they attend weddings. The church members become their friends and a substitute family.

They even gossip about other church members. Eventually they compete and certain conflicts arise just like they did a generation ago in the rural community. Likes and dislikes develop and people sort out groups or cliques within the church. It becomes a comfortable kind of structure that gives the uprooted person a community. It is important.

The remarried person may especially need this. It is not uncommon for a divorce and new marriage to automatically cut off social, community, and family ties. Even if these ties to the past are not destroyed, they are rearranged. Loneliness and feelings of isolation can be horribly painful, and they can be destructive of the new marriage. The remarried persons can find new community, new family, and new friends in the church. The church is particularly well-equipped to do this.

The church can help because the church gives people a place and opportunity for worship. I recognize that public worship services are often ineffective, poorly planned, and poorly done. But there is more to worship than a spectator/performance kind of thing. Certainly a public worship service involves the leadership of certain selected people. We expect our worship to be enhanced by a thoughtful sermon. We expect music that speaks to our heart. Corporate and private prayer are part of that worship and sincere worship leaders try to plan and conduct services that benefit the members of the congregation.

At times those who direct the worship seem to be unusually inspired, and the sermon, music, and prayers have a soaring, blessed effect on the participants. We all need this. There must be some "glory" in our worship. At every service in every church there is someone who has been lifted and inspired. We are never sure who is being touched in a positive way, but we can be sure that someone is.

At other times, perhaps most often, at least too often, the service does not seem inspired. There is sameness, routine. But even when the "performers" are not at their best, and even when the service seems flat and plagued by a slowly-moving clock, there is some value to "being in worship."

I know after more than twenty-five years of conducting worship services twice each Sunday, fifty-two weeks a year, that there is value in worship for the worshiper. Lives are often shaped, burdens taken away. Desperation is replaced by hope, weakness replaced by strength, and failing men find courage. Hate and bitterness give way to hope and forgiveness. Our mortality puts on immortality. I am not a fool. I would not have spent the best years of my life leading worship services if I thought worship was useless. There are too many people whose lives have been changed! I have personally seen too much good come out of worship to dismiss it as an optional, casual experience. I believe that people need to worship God. Their church is open for that purpose, and the worship services are designed to bring God and man together. This dimension of our humanity must be satisfied. We are spiritual creatures and we do need to worship. The church can help because the church offers worship opportunity. The remarried person needs to worship. And worship is part of the business of the church.

# *"Be careful about your reasons"*

When I was called as a pastor in 1948, my primary concerns related to the "official" things that Baptist pastors did in our culture. I knew that I would be expected to preach two sermons every Sunday, conduct funerals, baptize converts, serve communion, and conduct wedding ceremonies. I also knew that pastors visited the sick, called on prospects for church membership, and attended a lot of committee meetings.

I was not only surprised, but poorly prepared, when it soon became apparent that family counseling was a primary role of the pastor. It was nearly inconceivable to me that adults would seek my advice about family problems. I was a teenager, single, a college freshman, and completely inexperienced about marriage and child-rearing. Years later I realized that they recognized most of those limitations, but they were desperate for anyone to listen and advise.

Although I knew my limitations in education and experience, I was willing to listen and to give some guarded advice. It was a learning process for me. I am sure that I made a great many mistakes and gave a lot of people bad advice, but it was the best that I could do and I didn't have many alternatives. So I learned.

In marriage counseling during those first two years in that first church, I concluded that most of the people who came to me had married for the wrong reasons. The roots of their existing marriage problems went back to their reasons for marriage. People who marry for the wrong reasons will have the wrong expectations. They will get the wrong results. They soon find that marriage is a complex relationship and is a poor answer to a problem. When people decide to remarry after one marriage failure, they must be careful about their reasons for that decision.

"I always felt like I was rattling around in the apartment," Mac said. "I was never good alone. I had grown up with brothers and sisters, grandparents and neighbors going in and out of our house. My mother called it the bus station. There was noise. Tension. Activity. There were times when I was a boy that I craved privacy. Sometimes I could go off by myself, but not often. Maybe I didn't want it that much. There were always people around when I was in the service and in college. Then I married. We lived with her parents for a few months. Then we had two children. All of my life there have been people around. Now there is no one.

"I know that there is talk about being lonely in a crowd. That is true. You can be lonely in a crowd. Or the streets. In an office. In a church. Or at a football game. But the ultimate loneliness is aloneness. The alone person blasts a radio. Keeps the T.V. on all of the time. Goes to bed with a radio or a record playing. Gets a pet, or ten pets. Eventually the alone person begins talking to himself. When the prison official puts a guy in solitary confinement, he knows that he is going to break him, if not kill him, with aloneness.

"That aloneness is so terrible to me. I have decided that I will marry again. Being married to anyone is better than being alone. I will try to make a sensible choice, but I am not going to be that choosy. I am not going to live alone any longer!"

Mac has his reason. It is an understandable one. Many divorced people have made that same journey into aloneness and they don't like it. Not everyone wants people around all of the time. Some people enjoy privacy and independence. They do not need people; in fact, having someone around is unpleasant and intruding.

But most people can understand Mac's feelings. Being alone is painful and miserable.

If Mac finds a woman who wants to cure aloneness, they might make a marriage work. Perhaps two lonely people can be satisfied with nothing but human presence. Some people find a roommate for that reason; both people are able to go their separate ways and pursue their separate interests without emotional involvement. This is a difficult option if two people decide on marriage. It will be impossible to find some important parts of marriage if all either partner wants is a presence. Although fear of aloneness is understandable, it is not a reason for marriage.

Loneliness is a first cousin to aloneness, although they are not the same thing. Charles is lonely.

"I was married for eight years. One of the reasons that we divorced was loneliness. Edna, my first wife, and I had problems communicating and sharing. I know that sounds trite, but it was true. I am the kind of person who tells everything. As a boy I told my parents everything. They encouraged me, they corrected me, but they always listened. I could come in from school and tell them everything that had happened and they would listen. They always seemed interested. When Edna and I married, I tried the same thing with her for months, but she wasn't really interested. She didn't listen. She didn't compliment or criticize. She just didn't care.

"I know that I didn't listen to her either. She was a talker. She didn't talk as much as I do or about the same things. I thought that my life was more interesting and my stories more important than hers. Actually my life was more interesting. She never was into my life. She didn't want to be. And I was never into her life.

"Our interests were so different. Our careers, our hobbies, our entertainment were all different. We did have the same beliefs about child rearing, about church, and we agreed on most moral questions. But I was lonely with Edna and I'm more lonely now. I want to tell some-one about the changing colors of a tree on our street. I want to talk about my secretary's new boyfriend and I want to complain to someone about my secretary's tardi-ness. I want to admit my doubts and failures to someone who will sympathize and understand. It is important that someone listen to my ideas, even if they are just daydreams. Occasionally I have a success that I want to share with someone who is proud of me. A person needs a compliment.

"I'm going to marry again," Charles says. He has no one in mind. He hasn't met the "right" person yet. But he has made the decision to remarry because he is lonely.

"I simply can no longer endure the loneliness," Jerry explodes. I am reasonably successful in my work, but there is no one at home who cares. When I come in I want to tell someone about my ailments. I want to blow off to someone about my disappointments, but there isn't anyone at home who cares. My work is satisfying, but there is something missing about a job when there is no family to share it.

"The house is quiet. There are no noises except the television and the humming sounds of appliances. I lived for a dozen years with a wife who talked and with two small children. Do you realize how quiet it is when those sounds are gone? I go to sleep with the radio, wake up to the radio just to get some sound in the house.

"I eat by myself too much and I don't like to eat by myself. No one likes to eat alone often. Food and con-versation go together. So I don't eat at the right times, I don't eat the right food. I'm hungry but I'm not hungry.

"The other night there was a tornado in our area. It was a horrible thing. People were killed and millions of dollars in property was destroyed. We didn't have any electric power. People in our city were terrified. I lis-tened to the battery radio and huddled under a table. Sure I was frightened. And I was worried about my ex-wife and my kids. I knew that her new husband would take care of them. So I sat under that table and cried. Not from fear, but from a horrible loneliness. The next morning my mother called to see if I was OK. No one else called, because no one else cared.

"It's hard to sleep when you're lonely. I've tried it with the lights off. I have counted sheep, read in bed, watched the late T.V. shows, drunk warm milk, and gone to the health clubs. I get so tired that I'm punchy, but sleeping when you're lonely is tough. There is just no way to overcome loneliness except by being with people who care."

Jerry and his wife had a bad marriage. He does not regret the divorce, but he cannot adjust to the loneliness. It is not so much that he misses his wife; he just can't endure being alone. Even the arguments and tension in his marriage were not as distressing as the loneliness of his divorce. Jerry will marry again.

Jerry, Charles and Mac all face the most common distress of divorce and they reach the same conclusion. The answer to loneliness is marriage. But there is more to marriage than a cure for loneliness. It is possible that two lonely people can make happiness out of a marriage. But it is a risk. There must be more reason for marriage than loneliness.

"By the time I was a junior in college, I had decided that I wanted to be married when I was graduated," Kay tells me. "Most of the other girls were engaged or pinned. Looking back I realize that this was ironic. We were the generation of free-thinking students. We were independent. We rebelled against everything that was establishment. We were big on demonstrations. We were big on living together and casual sex. We drank, fooled with drugs, and made fun of a marriage license as just 'a piece of paper.' With all of that talk, we planned to be married by the time we got the 'piece of paper' that made us college graduates.

"No one talked about it. It was a subtle kind of pressure. I remember that my grandmother, who married at sixteen, used to say that a girl in the mountains was expected to be married at sixteen. I thought that was ridiculous! How could the social pressure in a little mountain town force her into marriage at sixteen? But that was exactly what happened to me when I was a student in a large, sophisticated university.

"Now I know that I made that decision when I was twenty. I decided to get married because my girlfriends were all going to be married. Even the ones who were big on freedom and casual sex were planning to get married. I wasn't going to be left out. After you decide to marry, then you must decide on the person. I decided that Lawson was the person that I wanted to marry.

"It was a good choice. Lawson had a good future. He was an ambitious student. He wasn't the brightest guy in the school, but he wasn't dull either. He wanted to be an attorney. He was attentive and polite to me. We had similar standards, our family life and rearing were compatible. We enjoyed each other. There were some differences but I refused to acknowledge them. If Lawson had any doubts, he never expressed them. We dated for more than a year, were properly married, and everyone assumed that it was all just perfect.

"It was a mismatch. Lawson and I got along all right. We never screamed and yelled. We never had fights. We went to church together. We went out together. We were both very conscious of what people thought and we did all of the correct and proper things to maintain our reputation in the community and the church. Although we never admitted it until just prior to the divorce, Lawson and I were always conditioned and controlled by what people thought.

"The simple truth was that we did not love each other. At least I did not love Lawson. I respected him. I liked him. But I felt like he was a brother, eventually an uncle, that I lived with. I did not love him. Maybe he gave me all of the love that he was capable of giving, but it was not enough. It was never enough. I married Lawson because people my age were all getting married, and that isn't enough, even if it's a nice guy like Lawson.

"Now I've been divorced from Lawson for eight months and I'm feeling the same kind of pressure," Kay continues. "Our society is not designed for single adults. All of my friends are married. My church is designed for married people. The T.V. commercials are pointed toward married people. The single woman is an oddity. There is no place where I fit in comfortably. I am the divorcee. The single adult."

Kay is considering remarriage for the same reason that she married the first time. Society seems to expect adults to be married. This kind of social pressure may be subtle or overt, but it is there. A person like Kay, who is especially conscious of social pressure and her image, is sensitive to her single status. It makes her uncomfortable. She doesn't like it. And although she says the right things about love and marriage, she is strongly inclined to marry again to gain social approval as a married woman in a society that is most comfortable with married people. Kay's reason for remarriage is understandable, but it is not reason enough for another marriage.

The church contributes to this desire to remarry. Consider Tom:

"I just would have never believed that this could have happened to me. My parents took me to this church when I was a child. Some of my earliest and best memories of being a boy are built around this church. I can remember former pastors, singing hymns, even counting the number of pieces in the stained glass windows."

Tom continues, "I was baptized in this church. My high school baccalaureate service was in this church. Mother's funeral was in this church. Why, my wedding was in this church.

"A considerable part of my life was invested in this place. I've given my time to meetings, boards, and volunteer work. One year I donated more money here than I spent on my house. There was no question ever in my mind that I would die as an active and respected member of this church."

Tom is hurt. His hurt is profound and honest. After his divorce his church life changed. It was nothing dramatic or harsh; it was subtle, but very real. The people in the church no longer felt comfortable around Tom. They were awkward and they said things that put him on edge. Some of the things were painful.

They did not talk about his divorce. They were embarrassed to discuss his divorce with him, and if he made some reference to being single they changed the subject. They were extremely self-conscious about Tom's divorce. Tom had known people would treat him differently; he thought he was prepared for that. And he knew that some people would be suspicious of him. But he can't help being angry.

"At the very time that I most needed Christian friends, at the time I most needed someone to talk to, to listen to, to laugh with. At that very time they ignored me.

"I have waited around after church until the janitor turned out the last light hoping someone would talk, or invite me to their house for a cup of coffee, but they are all in too much of a hurry. I've gone to the pastor and asked for a job, something to do that would put me with other people, but he never finds one. At first I would call some of the men up expecting some conversation, if not an invitation for a golf game, but the conversation was brief and perfunctory.

"I guess some of them are afraid of me. Some of them think they are better than I am. Some condemn me. Regardless of their reasoning, they have let me down. They have failed me. They have hurt me.

"All of this kind of thing makes me realize that remarriage is the only answer. If I am to regain any status in the church and community, I must have a wife," Tom concludes. His problems as a single man are real, but remarriage is not the answer. There is more to marriage than regaining status in the church and society, although status is important.

Some young people marry because they want to have sex without inhibition. Their sex drive is one of the primary reasons some of them marry. Sex is also one of the primary reasons for remarriage.

"I don't know about other people and their sex life; all I know is that my divorce has left me frustrated and starved for sex," Carolyn told me. "I suppose that most divorced people immediately fall into love affairs after their divorce. If they do, I can understand it. But it is not that casual or easy for me; I must feel something for the person to have sex with him. I can't find anyone that I feel for. And I'm about to go nuts."

It is very difficult for divorced people to turn off their sex desires after the divorce is decreed. During their marriage sex has been an important part of their life. Even if their sex life has been controversial and difficult, there has been some sex activity. Now that has changed.

"I have fantasies. I dream about sex and about sex with a variety of people. It shocks me. I have tried to turn it off. I don't read books or articles that would stimulate me, and I've gone the opposite way and deliberately read pornography and attended sex movies. I have tried to ignore my body and I have tried masturbation. Nothing helps. I'm just miserable and this disgusts me. No one would have ever believed that sex would drive me up a wall, but that is literally what is happening to me. I'm climbing the walls."

Too often divorced persons with serious sexual frustration decide that marriage is the answer to their dilemma. And of course marriage is the best and most acceptable way to express love through sex. Although some divorced people do engage in a series of sex affairs, most of them want the permanency and approval that marriage involves.

They find that casual sex is not fulfilling or satisfying.

They learn that their sexual frustration is more than a physical or biological urge. It is more than hunger or thirst, although they have been told that sex is a physical desire and that it can be satisfied like hunger and thirst.

The divorced person who goes through a procession of casual sex affairs complicates his or her life and loneliness. He or she discovers that the real hunger is to be loved and to love and that casual sex is a phony substitute. Some discover this in time to convert that life style, and instead of participating in a series of "one night stands" they settle down to look for and wait for love.

Sexual frustration is one of the reasons people marry again. This is understandable. Sex is powerful in people and it is especially important to the formerly-married who have enjoyed sex in their previous marriage. Although it is understandable, it is not reason enough to marry again.

Jean has been divorced for nearly two years. She wants to remarry because she believes, with reason, that her children need a father. It is not uncommon for divorced people with children to reach that kind of conclusion about another marriage.

"I have three children by two husbands," Jean began her story. "I married the first time when I was seventeen and by the time I was twenty I had two children. My first husband, Jack, and I neither were ready to accept all of the responsibilities that went with marriage and two children. We were just immature. We felt that we had been denied the normal things that teenagers enjoy. So, in our early twenties, with two kids at home, we both lived like teenagers. Both sets of parents helped take care of the children while we were running around. Looking back, it all seems so silly and childish.

"Jack rarely came home and finally he just moved in with this other girl. Incidentally, she was a teenager. I didn't really care. I moved in with my parents. They were taking care of the children anyway. I was glad for them to assume all of that responsibility and they did. It was probably better for the children too.

"About three years later, after the divorce from Jack, I married Gil. He was older. He represented some security to me. He drove a big car and wore nice clothes. He was quite a talker. He could talk me into anything. Gil said that he would be a good father to my children. Gil and I had a baby the first year of our marriage.

"It didn't take long for me to realize that Gil was a con man. He used me. He used the children. He used the church. He used his friends. Gil made a lot of money at times and he would lose it just as quickly. He was always into some big deal. He sold all kinds of things, usually some kind of stock or shares in small businesses. For three years it was boom or bust. Then things began to catch up with Gil. He was indicted on more than twenty counts of fraud, embezzlement and bad checks. People in the church went to bat for him and he was given a suspended sentence. Then he ripped off the very church members who had bailed him out. He finally went to prison.

"Now I have three children. No money. My husband is in prison. I feel ashamed and disgraced. My parents are angry and embarrassed. But the church did give me support. Some of the "welfare" programs not only fed us but I was able to train for a job. Now I work and can keep the family clothed and fed.

"But my kids need a father. All children need a father. I am firmly convinced that any child reared in a one-parent family is going to be hurt and handicapped. Children need two parents!

"And we need another wage earner. I've been able to get by financially, but that is all. I want my children to have at least some of the same things that other kids have. We are not destitute, but we are surely 'low income.' Another wage earner would certainly change our financial situation. That may not be a good motive, but that is the way it is."

Jean continues, "I have some things figured out. Sure I am lonely. I would like to marry again because I'm lonely and I don't like being a single adult. But I can live with it. The children are another story. The children need a father. They need a man around because they need to relate well to a man. The oldest boy needs a father to imitate, to advise him, to take him to ball games. I feel inadequate in disciplining them and advising them. I know that kids from one-parent families often get into trouble.

"There is just too much in child-rearing for me to face alone. Soon the children will be teenagers. That scares me to death. I don't think I can cope with them when they are teenagers. They need a man to be there.

"Another thing. They were all hurt and embarrassed more than I was when Gil went to prison. It scared them. A new father that they can respect will help heal the wounds they got from Gil. I owe them that."

Jean's concern for her children is commendable. It is often expressed by divorced parents. Boys and girls do need the security and example of a two-parent family. Many stepparents do adjust to new children and children do adjust to a new parent.

In talking with couples who contemplate remarriage and who have children, this business of stepparenting is one of the things I hear them talk about. Couples getting married for the first time must consider the question of children, unborn children. Couples who plan marriage and who have children must give careful consideration to their children.

We can understand the desire of a parent to marry again and provide the children with a two-parent family. But that is not reason enough for marriage. The parent who has already decided once that he or she could not hold a bad marriage together for children will not be able to hold another marriage together just because children need two parents.

People want to remarry. There are reasons for remarriage. But there is only one reason that is valid and that will make the new marriage work. The two people must love.

# "The greatest is love"

Remarriage can work if it is based upon love. Although love is one of the most used words in our generation, it is still the most important feeling that humans have. It is the most important factor in any marriage. Love is not cheap romance. Love is not passing emotion. Love is not glib or casual. By contrast, love is essential in human relationships, especially marriage. It is freely given, freely accepted, and is absolutely necessary in marriage.

Although love is being used to describe all kinds of relationships, and although love descriptions are on banners, posters, bumper stickers, and greeting cards, no one can improve upon the biblical definitions of love. Love is "in" in this generation, but there is still a need for the definitive understanding of love stated in the Bible.

Love in the Bible is not an abstract theological concept. It is not a word to be mouthed as an ideal for Christians. Too often Christians apply love in an abstract, idealistic way that has absolutely no relationship to day-by-day living. We talk about God loving the world and loving sinners, but we do not really believe that God actively loves a particular sinner. We talk about God loving little children, about loving our enemies, about loving the church. All of this sounds good. Unfortunately we overlook the little child next door, the man at work who gets the promotion we wanted, or our own church. Tragically, we omit the idea of love from marriage. We are embarrassed when a man says he loves a woman. Somehow that doesn't seem to fit into our religious concepts. Loving sinners is OK, but loving a woman sounds out of place in contemporary religious jargon. No marriage can work unless there is love between the marriage partners.

We are told that the Greeks in Jesus' time used three words that are translated "love." We cannot improve on those words for man-woman love. Married love must include *philos*, *eros*, and *agape*.

Every elementary school child learns that Philadelphia, the cradle of our nation, was the "city of Brotherly Love." The founders understood something about *philos*. In our generation we might call "brotherly love" companionship or friendship. Every marriage must have friendship. *Philos*.

A man and woman who love will enjoy one another. They will be friends. They like one another. They want to be together and they enjoy being together. They have fun. They share secrets. A kind of profound companionship develops. It is comfortable, familiar, and essential to their happiness. They know what the loved one is thinking, they can anticipate and predict behavior because they care enough to observe carefully their lover's moods, actions, and general behavior.

My mother had a plaque, which I have in my study now, that says "a friend is one who knows all about you and loves you just the same." This is *philos*. Understanding. A lover understands the one he loves, and that kind of love accepts. Understanding, if it is genuine, always accepts. This is the difference between knowledge and understanding.

Too often in man-woman relationships we omit understanding and acceptance. We marry people in order to change them. There are married people who exhaust themselves during the entire marriage experience trying to change their partner. This kind of nagging and harassment would be unthinkable with a friend, but becomes customary in a marriage. The man-woman relationship loses every attribute of friendship, *philos*, and becomes an unending conflict of will. The insistence and persistence of some married people to change the one they "love" is frightening and is ultimately destructive to the relationship.

*Philos* requires an effort at understanding. We have the right to question the behavior or the attitudes of one we love. The questioning is always designed to gain understanding; it is never to accumulate data for the next fight or to provide arguments for the next assault in the unending effort to change the one we love.

With understanding there must be acceptance. When we learn why our lovers act and feel the way they do, we can accept them that way. I am astonished continuously in counseling at the number of irritations that people accumulate. Some husbands and wives do not want their partners to change in only one or two areas; they demand a complete overhaul and personality change. Acceptance means that we will take them as they are. We should not marry because we "can make a silk purse out of a sow's ear." We should not marry because of potential. We should not marry because someone is pliable and will be easy to control. Acceptance is "Just As I Am" or, as Cromwell said it, "Warts and all."

*Philos* is more than acceptance, *philos* is trust. Nothing can destroy a friendship more than a breach of trust. Nothing is more essential to friendship than trust. Surely man and woman in love will trust each other. Trust is telling your lover things that are intimate and private, that you would tell no one unless you trusted them. Trust is having absolute confidence that the deepest feelings of your heart will be respected as sacred.

*Philos* means trust so profound that fears can be freely admitted. Often people say that they have kept their fears locked up tightly because they were embarassed to admit them to anyone. These hidden fears become an enormous burden upon the person who has found no one to trust, no one to love.

I think this kind of trust also involves judgment. We can get advice and counsel from one we trust. There are many decisions about our work or other areas of life that do not involve the competence or knowledge of our trusted one. A chemical engineer may face an important decision that his wife, who is a social worker, has no professional knowledge about. But as his trusted lover she can hear him out and give him personal advice, admittedly highly subjective, because she does love him. The advice may not be valuable, or even right. He may not take it. But that is not important to either one of them. What is important is the trust. Often excluding our loved one from decisions is interpreted, correctly, as a lack of trust.

Trust has to do with integrity. Integrity is being yourself. I do not have to "put on" with a person that I love and trust. There is nothing phony about integrity. No masks. No hidden agendas. If I am to ever be honest, I will be honest with a person that I love.

The person of integrity will admit his limitations. He will say, "I don't know." The person of integrity can admit his mistakes. He will admit that he has been wrong. A man and woman in love can admit these limitations to each other. They are not afraid that the limitations will weaken or destroy their love. This kind of love is not built upon strength or perfection; it is built upon the kind of respect that is produced by integrity.

*Philos* love is acted out. It is expressed as well as felt. Some people are romantic idealists. They have a poetic, soap opera, nearly adolescent conception of love. To them, love is a kind of dream—always pursued, always elusive. And there is that element of dream in love. But love is more than that. The person who loves acts it out with another person.

The Greeks in Jesus' time had another word for love—*eros*. Movie makers and sex magazine publishers have overused *erotic*, and we have all become self-conscious about the word and even the concept. But a marriage must have *eros* to it. It is an important element.

It is possible to have sex without love, but it is impossible to have love without sex. By the very nature of our creation, sex is the most intimate and personal, the most urgent and satisfying way to express love. Sex has always been more than reproduction. Sex has always expressed more than the desire for babies. It is always more than a physical urge or a biological necessity. Sex is more than intercourse. It is more than the "sex act." Sexual attraction, sexual desire, involves all of the physical aspects of the relationship between a man and a woman. Love always involves physical attraction, and when sexual intercourse is impossible or is postponed, there can still be erotic love or physical appeal. We inhibit and limit sex when it is confined to intercourse.

A man and woman contemplating marriage should have *eros*. There must be sex appeal. An honest person admits that sex appeal is more than beauty and charm. There are some men and women who are obviously attractive by most standards. They are physically appealing. They look good. They are well-groomed, well-dressed, and they have "charisma." People are attracted to them. This is a kind of abstract sex appeal and is often evidenced in public figures, movie stars, or television personalities. Some have more than others.

When children first come into puberty, they go through a stage where they envy and imitate attractive public people or certain kids at school. During these adolescent years, however, they learn that sex appeal, or attractiveness, is not the same to everyone. Most of the boys in the eighth grade will agree that Susie is pretty, but one by one each of the boys focuses on one of the other girls. Their tastes will change and develop, and Sally will have an admirer too, although no one but her admirer will think Sally is pretty and attractive.

Our sex attractions are different. We are not all emotionally interested in or drawn to the same person or the same kind of person. There is a variety of taste. *Eros* can not be explained or accurately analyzed. It is not a rational thing. *Eros* is more feeling than fact. It is more heart than head.

I believe that sex is one of the strongest human desires

and that this drive affects our personality and behavior more than most of us realize or admit. Conservative church people normally have real problems handling their sex drives. They have been taught that somehow sex is sinful, or at least extremely private and embarassing. They do not cope with the urge for sex very well and they even have problems with sex in marriage.

Sexual hang-ups affect the salesman's ability to sell, the physician's skills in the hospital, the teacher's work in the classroom. Sex frustrations are common to the butcher, baker, and candlestick maker. Only God knows how sex has affected war and peace, legislation, research and education, the arts, religion, and mental health.

Church meetings and church life have often pivoted around sex. It is more than Episcopalian ordination of women. It is more than Roman Catholic pronouncements about birth control or married priests. It is more than the Baptist pastor running off with the organist. It is more than scandal, controversy, or morals. The church has tried for centuries to explain and control this tremendous human drive. The church has tried to channel sex into chastity, or reproduction, or self-control. Unfortunately we have not successfully tied sex into love. We have been too self-conscious and too rigid to acknowledge that sex is part of love.

Sex without love is possible. In our society it is probable. There is no doubt that we are a sexually-preoccupied people. As we escaped from "puritanism" we became excessively "liberal" about sex. Television, movies, books and private conversation have become permeated, if not dominated, by sex.

Puritanism was a distortion. Puritanism tried to ignore sex. Puritanism implied that sex was bad, embarassing, and wasn't a fact of life. So "polite" people did not talk about it. They did not admit it. As a result we had generations of people who handled their sexual impulses poorly because sex was surrounded by myth and untruth. No one perpetuated that error with more zeal and more effect than the church. Conservative church people still perpetuate those myths and distortions.

A new generation overreacted and perpetuated another distortion. The current distortion is that sex is unrelated to love and commitment. Although the current sex peddlers try to make sex casual and common, their obsessive preoccupation with sex betrays their distortion. Sex has always been more than a casual relationship.

To correct any distortion, the only answer is the truth. The truth is that sex is a part of love. Any sex education that ignores love is incomplete and inadequate. The public schools and certain sex behavior forums often ignore the emotional and "feeling" part of sex. Consequently, this kind of sex education is reduced to the mechanical and physical aspects of sex.

There is a new, and needed, emphasis upon the biology of sex. People do need to know what is happening physically when they are stimulated or involved in sex activity. And there is a deluge of information, or misinformation, about the physiological aspects of sex. Volumes have been written, by clinicians and pornographers and every kind of "expert" in between those extremes, about the psychology of sex. Again, this is important to some degree, because there is a psychology to sex. Desire, frustration, joy—all of these feelings are common to the human sex experience. They need to be understood and exploration is important.

But there is the biblical idea of love that relates to sex. It is overlooked or put down in our current sexology. Even biblical writers, expositors, clergy, and religious counselors seem reluctant to put sex and love together. We say to children that sex should wait for love, but we are embarassed and hesitant to explain what we mean. We usually tell young people about sex and love because we are trying to keep them from having premarital sex. We rarely explain that sex not only expresses love between man and woman, but it is the essence of that love.

Our language gives us away. We usually speak of sex in terms other than love. I will not list, but do remind, that we have a chain of words for sex. Most of this language is offensive to people, especially to church people. We usually refer to "four-letter words" and assume that these four-letter "sex words" are obscene. We should use the four letter word "love" in our sex vocabulary.

It is common and acceptable to speak of people "going to bed together." And that is all that happens in some sex activity. It is also common to say that someone has "made" someone else, or that someone is on the "make." The clear implication is that someone maneuvers, seduces, or entices an unwilling person into sex. This happens and happens often, even in marriage. But people in love do not have to be "made." Sex and love are coexistent and together they imply a willingness, even mutual desire, that is contrary to being "made."

Or we say that someone "makes love to" someone else. There is a sound of attack in that phrase. People in love make love together. Make love with someone, not to someone. Our language betrays our discomfort with sex and love.

Is *eros* an exclusive expression of love? If you love someone in an erotic, physical, sexual way, does this exclude the option of extramarital interests and extramarital affairs? Can a man or woman who is genuinely in love find all of their sexual needs in one person, or is it natural and normal to be sexually interested in another person besides the one you love? We all recall the discussion that followed Candidate Jimmy Carter's comments in 1976 about lust and extramarital sex.

Men and women are always aware of other men and women. You can be in love and still admire another person. You can enjoy their company. You can find them attractive, interesting, intriguing, and pleasant. They can flatter you. They can respond to your attention. All of this is possible, normal, and certainly is not immoral, nor is it a betrayal of your love. These kinds of relationships often develop into affairs and sex liaisons. But not always. There is the opportunity for these relationships to become affairs, but the person who is secure in his or her love doesn't need it. They can relate comfortably with the opposite sex, but they do not need the sex affair.

It is more difficult than it should be for opposite sexes to have comfortable friendships. Church people are especially vulnerable because of their suspicions. This kind of suspicion jeopardizes many constructive and healthy relationships that could be mutually helpful.

This is not to suggest that the person who loves would be indifferent or unconcerned about any kind of opposite sex relationships. It is very human, and very correct, for a person who loves to want his or her partner as an exclusive lover. It is not normal and not loving to share that love in any intimate way with someone else. Jealousy is not suspicion.

Sex expresses love in an intensely personal way. People who have sexual hang-ups have not been able to express that love in the right way, at the right time, or to the right person. The dimension of love in sex is the very ingredient that modifies and justifies sex. Love is the handle that controls sex. This kind of sex has smell, taste, feeling, language, urgency, peace, comfort, and security. It is tender and passionate, reckless and considerate, impulsive and calculated. But most of all, it is committed and expressed.

*Eros* is love. The man and woman who plan to make a marriage work must be that kind of lovers.

The ultimate word for love in the Bible is *agape*. We have all been taught that *agape* describes God's love for us. This is a lofty concept, and some churchmen assume that this kind of love is just beyond the human capacity. But the Bible writers do not restrict *agape* to God's love for us; they use it often to describe human love. One of the most human love verses applies to husbands and wives (Eph. 5:25). I believe that *agape* is necessary and possible in husband-wife relationships.

*Agape* doesn't keep score. This kind of love is never

restricted by "you do this for me, and I'll do that for you." Of course, any constructive relationship has some give and take, some compromise to it. There is a difference in compromise and accommodation and making points in the marriage. *Agape* precludes making points. It does not even consider scorekeeping. The lover does not try to please the one he loves to get something he wants; he tries to please his lover simply because he loves her. Collecting vouchers, cashing in chips, being repaid for kindness is foreign to *agape*. God doesn't love us because he is in debt to us; he loves us because he loves us.

*Agape* is not conditional. Love does not depend upon the other person's behavior. I hear people say that they learned "not to love" someone because of something that person did or said, or because of a type of lifestyle or behavioral change. People change. They always are changing. Love does not depend upon sameness or constancy of behavior. Love can be constant when the object of love is not constant. *Agape* is not given with strings attached. It is not given partially, so that it can be easily or quickly withdrawn. Because it is not conditional, it should be given carefully, if not reluctantly, and never casually.

There is something timeless about love. Lincoln had "Love is Eternal" inscribed in his wedding band gift to Mary Todd. Lovers of every generation have said this. The love of God is never limited to time. *Agape* is eternal. All of us have watched lovers go through the years together. There have been good times and bad, sickness and health, poverty, pain, excitement, and joy. Somehow these people have grown closer together, and their love has been sweeter with the passing years. The passing days enhanced and deepened the love. That love endured all of the vicissitudes of time and brought the two lovers at forty or eighty to the end of life with an enviable peace. In a transient world, nothing is more appealing than a relationship that endures like that. Love has that endurance, because love is eternal.

All of my life I have seen this illustrated. I have known people of unusual achievement and success who always share their good fortune eagerly with the one they love. That mutual joy has been the supreme compliment and satisfaction that accompanies the good news. And we have all known the high achiever, who has known the emptiness of success because there was no lover to share it.

I have known people who have suffered beyond normal human endurance. They have had so much pain and failure that you expect them to simply give up and cave in. But they bravely bear that portion of life, because they have a lover to share every misfortune and setback. They have never felt alone, because they always had their lover. They can take anything that comes because of that love. This is agape. Love that is not conditional; it does not depend upon time or circumstances. It is eternal and timeless by nature.

*Agape* is helping. God helps us because he love us. God doesn't put us down, he doesn't exploit our weaknesses, he doesn't get on our neck when we're down. Love between a man and woman means helping. This is more than companionship and sharing; it is a conscious effort to help. It is being aware of need, aware of weakness, aware of fear. Aware of frustration, anger, or despair. The lover tries to help. This is not condescending or patronizing. It is genuine caring. It is expressed and it works.

*Agape* is giving. This may be the most important description of love. The lover gives, with no thought of return. He does not invest; he gives. He does not consider the bottom line or the pay off. He gives gifts. He gives time. He gives talent. He gives himself. He wants to give laughter and pleasure. He wants to give security and comfort. He wants to give help and consistency. He gives his body, his mind, his resources, himself. His giving is always willing. He wants to do it. He does not have to be tricked, or cajoled, or threatened. He gives eagerly.

The giving is sacrificial. It is extravagant. No one who

loves is cheap or parsimonious. No one who loves counts the cost. A lover gives it all. Love giving is always sacrificial because one who loves always gives all that he has and wants to give more. Nothing is withheld, nothing is hidden or protected.

Paul said that *agape* "is longsuffering. It is kind. Does not envy. Is not puffed up. Behaves. Doesn't seek its own way. Is not easily provoked. Thinks not evil. Rejoices in truth, not evil. It will bear anything, believe anything, hope for everything, and endure everything. It will never fail" (1 Cor. 13:5–8, Author's Paraphrase). This is all true. Love will never fail. It will always be present in a good marriage. Any marriage will work if the two people love one another.

Love is sitting together in a porch swing watching fireflies on a summer night. Love is leaning on each other while the baby fights for breath. Love is a memory of some private yesterday. Love is a smile that no one else understands. Love is pride in the other's personal achievement. Love is an ecstatic, impulsive sex act. Love is an unexpected gift in April. Love is finishing a sentence because you know what the other is going to say. Love is anticipating, and forgetting, a temper tantrum. Love is an accumulation of secrets. Love is crying together. Love is the way you hold hands. Love is respect and trust. Love is in the eyes—intensity, pain, excitement, desire, and mischief. Love is in the soul—longing, sharing, and satisfying. Love is hurting through death, but knowing that death never destroys love. Love is winning, always winning.

With that love, marriage—and remarriage—works.